CUNARD

QUEEN VICTORIA

A CELEBRATION OF TRADITION FOR
TWENTY-FIRST CENTURY OCEAN TRAVEL

PHILIP DAWSON

CONTENTS

Produced and designed by Ferry Publications trading as Lily Publications Ltd

PO Box 33, Ramsey, Isle of Man, British Isles, IM99 4LP

Tel: +44 (0) 1624 898446   Fax: +44 (0) 1624 898449

www.ferrypubs.co.uk   EMail: info@lilypublications.co.uk

Printed and bound by Gomer Press Ltd., Wales, UK +44 (0) 1559 362371 © Lily Publications 2010

First Published: May 2010

Second Edition: August 2010

Third Edition: August 2013

*The **Queen Victoria** arrives at Rotterdam, the first port of call on her inaugural Christmas markets cruise to Northern Europe. (Mike Louagie)*

INTRODUCTION

BY PHILIP DAWSON

Twenty years ago this spring (1990) my first book British Superliners of the Sixties was published – it was a design appreciation of P&O's *Oriana* and *Canberra*, and Cunard's *Queen Elizabeth 2* – arguably three of the more significant liners to be built in the twentieth century. For me this first book was an expression of my lifelong fascination with ships and something tantamount to a love affair with these three great British ladies in particular. Through this work I met many of the key people involved in the design and building of these ships, including the *Canberra*'s naval architect, John West, P&O Orient Line's naval architect David McKee, as well as the *QE2* architectural designers, Jon Bannenberg, James Gardner and Michael Inchbald, and dear Sir Hugh Casson, who was involved both with the *Canberra* and *QE2*, who was kind enough to write the book's foreword and has remained a mentor and source of inspiration to me.

When the *Oriana* and *Canberra* made their debut some thirty years earlier I was but a schoolboy, and can remember reading of these and pouring over the cut-away illustrations of them in Meccano Magazine for hours on end – ships such as these were then the promise of the future. Nearly ten years on, as a young man, I was equally fascinated by the *QE2*, her remarkable exterior appearance, sophisticated engineering and crisp internal modernity – but by that time we were being told that big passenger ships were becoming a thing of the past, and that she would probably be the last ever of her kind. There was absolutely

no foretelling then of the bright new age of unprecedented passenger-ship building that lay ahead, much less that there would ever be another North Atlantic liner built to carry on after the *QE2* would reach the inevitable end of her illustrious career.

Passenger ships today are very different from what they were in the time of those wonderful old British superliners. The dream of building these as large as supertankers is now a reality, and the style of life upon the ocean wave is more diverse and generally less formal in keeping with twenty-first century living ashore. With the debut of Cunard's *Queen Mary 2* in 2004, the future of Samuel Cunard's legendary North Atlantic liner service that has operated continuously since 1840 is assured for at least the next forty years – and now this latest flagship is being joined by the *Queen Victoria* and *Queen Elizabeth*, giving the venerable Cunard name one of the youngest and most technologically advanced fleets in the world. Yet these are designed to also celebrate the rich tradition of the Cunard institution and liner experience through its long and illustrious history of more than 170 years.

In the globalised milieu of business today, Cunard is now part of the international Carnival Group, the Line's current fleet is built in France and Italy. The steam turbine machinery of the old Queens has given way to energy-efficient gas turbine and diesel-electric power plants and to powerful azimuthing propeller pods. Cunard's three new Queens are the realisation of a childhood dream held by a

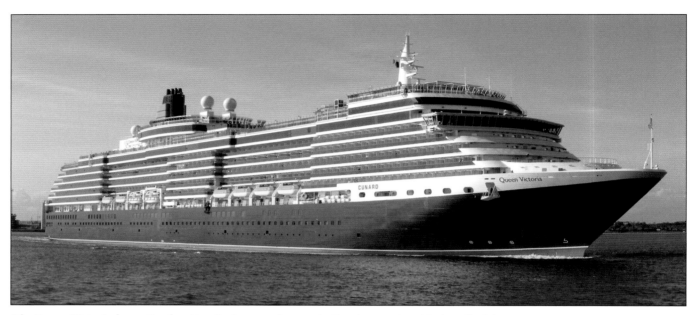

*The **Queen Victoria** leaves Southampton for her second season in European waters. (Andrew Cooke)*

nine-year-old boy named Stephen Payne who visited the *QE2* on a family outing in 1969 and set his mind then and there that there would indeed be more great passenger liners in the future and that he would make his career designing them. The interiors of *Queen Victoria* and *Queen Elizabeth* bear the refined creative signature of Teresa Anderson in her skilful rendering of an on-board atmosphere with a broad universal appeal that also conveys a strong impression of Cunard's own very special sense of history and ocean-going tradition.

I was delighted to be asked by Miles Cowsill of Ferry Publications to write books on *Queen Victoria* and *Queen Elizabeth* following the success of our commemorative work on *Queen Elizabeth 2*, co-authored with Bruce Peter and Ian Johnston. This is another opportunity to continue telling the story started with British Superliners two decades ago. It is part of an ongoing odyssey of learning and discovery of

ships, and the people who design, build, operate and sail in them. It is also the great privilege of being entrusted by our good friends at Cunard to tell their story and that of their remarkable ships and people.

Welcome aboard for this short voyage through the background to the *Queen Victoria*'s creation, the design and building of the ship herself and her entry into service at the end of 2007. We shall become familiar with the *Queen Victoria*'s accommodations, various public spaces and facilities, her cuisine, entertainment and other special services that give her the unique personality and character of a twenty-first century Cunard Queen.

I sincerely hope you enjoy the voyage.

Philip Dawson,
Toronto, June 2010

*The **Queen Victoria**, An interior view of the Café Carinthia, located on 2 Deck starboard of the Grand Lobby. (Mike Louagie)*

CHAPTER I

SETTING THE SCENE

CUNARD

QUEEN VICTORIA

Cunard's new *Queen Victoria* is first to follow in the great success of the Line's highly acclaimed liner *Queen Mary 2*, delivered three years earlier at the end of 2003 as a new fleet mate and ultimately a replacement for the much-loved *Queen Elizabeth 2*, herself dating from 1969. While *Queen Victoria* incorporates much from the new *QM2*, with the benefit of her proven service experience in particular, the *Queen Victoria* is herself remarkably different in character, reflecting also some of the Line's more traditional values, going back to the era of true *Grand Luxe* sea travel from even earlier than the venerable *Old Queens*, *Mary* and *Elizabeth*.

The *QE2* was originally built as a crisply modern expression of the very best in British architectural and interior design from the *Swinging Sixties* during which she was planned. The *QM2* followed in a contemporary ocean-going hotelier style with, as her co-ordinating interior architect, Andy Collier of SMC Design puts it, a "tip of the hat to tradition."[1] The *Queen Victoria* presents a predominantly traditional on-board atmosphere celebrating the popular notion of Cunard's illustrious history and background. Rather than endeavouring to reproduce period pieces from earlier times, this is achieved through generic classic styling in the public areas that asserts the desired atmosphere as a background for enjoyment of the experience in an

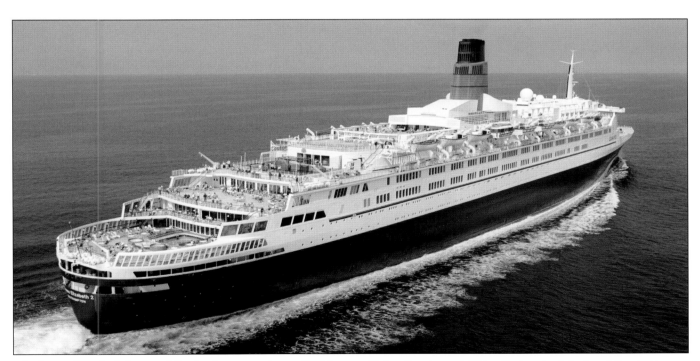

The **Queen Elizabeth 2** *at sea following her conversion to diesel power, with her Quarter and Upper Decks extended aft and the stockier funnel in traditional Cunard colours needed for the diesel uptakes. (FotoFlite)*

*The **Caronia**, formerly Norwegian America's **Vistafjord**, in Cunard's new traditional livery with a dark charcoal grey hull, underway in the River Forth. (Bruce Peter)*

otherwise entirely up-to-date cruise setting that meets today's lifestyle expectations.

The *Queen Victoria* is also a significant product of Carnival Corporate Shipbuilding, that serves the needs of the entire Carnival Group, as the parent of Cunard, Holland America, Costa and Carnival's own brands, along with P&O and Princess Cruises. With this comes the world's greatest mass of passenger shipbuilding know-how and experience, covering all the latest technological advances in power and propulsion, navigation and electronics, energy conservation and environmental friendliness. While providing for the distinct culture and flavour of each fleet and individual ship, this also builds upon a highly rationalised approach to all-important inner workings such as food and beverages, hotel services and laundry, stores and baggage handling that go on behind the scenes away from the passengers' gaze. Headquartered in Southampton, England, this is a veritable dynamo of shipbuilding activity that traces its origins back to

Carnival's first new ship, the *Tropicale*, completed nearly three decades ago in 1981.

In 2003, before the *QM2*'s inaugural season the following year, plans were already afoot at Carnival for the fourth hull in their upscale Vista-class series, of which the lead ship *Zuiderdam* was delivered to Holland America Line in November 2002, to be allocated to Cunard for completion in 2005 as part of a fleet redevelopment scheme to bring the Line into the same league as its competitors. Ultimately this ship ended up as P&O's *Arcadia*, with Cunard moving to a modified and slightly lengthened additional ship in the series delivered as the *Queen Victoria* two years later at the end of 2007.

Built as Cunard's second largest vessel after the *QM2*, this would definitely be a *Queen*-class addition to the fleet, though without herself necessarily being a full-fledged North Atlantic liner of the same power and structural stamina as the *QM2*. While the pundits speculated that stalwart Cunard names such as *Mauretania*, *Aquitania* or perhaps even *Berengaria*, might

*The **Queen Mary 2** being manoeuvred by tugs in the Loire Estuary during her sea trials in late 2003. (Cunard)*

be chosen, a *Queen*-sized Cunarder would have to be given a Queen's name, and thus it was that inevitably *Queen Victoria* came out on top as early as 2004 to be the most logical choice. The *QE2* was at the time still in service, then with no immediate prospect of being sold off and mustered out of the fleet. While the name *QM2* acknowledges the old *Queen Mary*'s enduring sojourn in a static role as a hotel and tourist attraction in Long Beach, California, there would be no need to qualify the new ship's name with a numeral, either Roman or Arabic, as Victoria's name has never been used by Cunard nor for any other merchant ship currently in existence.

Yet as the management and technical talent at Carnival, Cunard and the ship's Italian builders Fincantieri, dealt with the business of designing and building the new Cunarder, and their marketing colleagues started to promote the aura of the ultimate *traditional* cruise experience aboard an *iconic* Cunard liner[2] to the cruising public. Probably no one at the time

*The **Queen Mary 2**, showing her Commodore Club lounge, designed as a modern adaptation of the forward Cocktail Bar on the old **Queen Mary** in keeping with the new ship's more contemporary leitmotif. (Cunard)*

realised the significance of the long and illustrious reign of Queen Victoria, as the prosperous golden age into which the Cunard Line itself was born and lived through its adolescence.

*Cunard's **Queen Mary 2** and **Queen Elizabeth 2** are seen together at Fort Lauderdale, Florida as sisters from two separate generations. (Cunard)*

A child of the Victorian era

Eighteen-year-old Alexandrina Victoria, daughter of Prince Edward Augustus, Duke of Kent and Princess Victoria of Saxe Cobourg Saalfeld, became Queen of Great Britain and its overseas possessions on the morning of 20th June 1837 following her uncle, King William IV's death at the age of 71 from heart failure at 2:00 am that day. The throne had passed to Victoria because neither her father, nor his two siblings, had any other surviving legitimate children at the time of William's death. Victoria's reign of sixty-three years and seven months until her death on 22nd January 1901 is the longest in British history, covering a time of great prosperity and human achievement known as the Victorian era. As Britain had by then become a constitutional monarchy, where political and executive power is vested with an elected parliament who's prime minister generally advises the Monarch on matters of government and state, the presence of Victoria and her Prince Consort, Albert, was of an important rallying symbolic significance for the times.

The Victorian era also coincided with, and was part of, a broader phenomenon known as the Industrial Revolution, which brought about the greatest period of change experienced by human civilization since the agricultural and Neolithic Revolution that defined the beginning of our civilization more than ten thousand years ago.[3] Starting in the early nineteenth century, a transition was made from an agrarian economy with manual labour and draft-animal power to mining and machine-based manufacturing, originating in the textile and iron industries. From about the time of Queen Victoria's coronation the so-called Second Industrial Revolution was focused more on the growth of mass

*A painting of the tiny paddle steamer **Britannia** that inaugurated Cunard's regular transatlantic service in 1840, and apart from its suspension during times of war remains as a seasonal service to this day. (Author's collection)*

transport systems by rail, sea, and later road, as well as the building of infrastructure and production of consumer goods and other manufactured products for domestic and export markets. Combined, the Second Industrial Revolution and Victorian era were a remarkable period driven largely by the march of great economic, scientific, technical, social and intellectual progress.

There was great engineering progress in steam power, mechanisation and in the fabrication of machinery and other structures of iron and steel that brought with it the development of railways and steam shipping. These quickly progressed from their infancy as the technical curiosities first created by their inventors to becoming major industries and a way of life for many.

Transcontinental railways were built in Australia, Canada, the United States and across the sub-continent of India. The Suez Canal was built, creating a direct sea link between the Mediterranean and the Red Sea, greatly shortening the sailing distance from Britain and Europe to India, the Far East, Australia and New Zealand. Photography progressed from its experimental origins to the point where hand-held cameras and film processing were available to the public. Telegraph, and later wireless, brought about the vestigial beginnings of the real-time communications that are the basis of our networked and online world of the twenty-first century.

In 1839 two years after Victoria took the throne, Samuel Cunard (1787-1865), an enterprising Canadian merchant from Halifax, Nova Scotia, was awarded an Admiralty's contract to carry mail transatlantic by steamship between Liverpool, Halifax and Boston, with scheduled sailings every two weeks in both directions for eight months of the year for an annual fee of £50,000. Precedents had already been set for steam-powered Atlantic passages from as early as 1819, when the American paddle steamer *Savannah* crossed from the American city of Savannah to Liverpool in 27 days and 15 hours, during which her engines were only in use for 80 hours. Perhaps those earlier ventures with the best chance of being commercially viable were the British and American Steam Navigation Company and the Great Western Steamship Company, both founded in 1838, though remaining in service only until 1841 and 1846 respectively.

With steam there came a fundamental change in the shipping business that vessels "will positively sail full or not," on scheduled dates, instead of the existing sailing packet practice of waiting for a full cargo before sailing. While there was no way to determine actual voyage times under sail, constant speeds could be maintained aboard machine-powered ships, and their comings and goings thus scheduled on the same basis as railway timetables.

Four wooden paddle steamers were launched on the Clyde for Cunard, each with a measure of 1,135 gross tons (GT), a length of 69.6 metres, a speed of 9 knots, and modest accommodation for 115 passengers. The first of these, *Britannia*, made her maiden voyage to Halifax and Boston with only 63 passengers aboard, sailing from Liverpool on 4th July 1840, arriving in Halifax 12 days and 10 hours later on 17th July. The remaining three ships, *Acadia*, *Caledonia* and *Columbia*, were completed and came on-stream between August that year and the following January, bringing into being a transatlantic passenger and mail service of great regularity and reliability, and originating the longest-serving passenger shipping enterprise in history, continuing to the present day with Atlantic voyages being made now aboard the Line's *Queen Mary 2*.

The company was originally chartered in Liverpool as the British and North American Royal Mail Steam Packet Company. This rather formal and somewhat unwieldy title was shortened to "The Cunard" or simply Cunard in everyday usage, and has since formally become Cunard Line, or again simply Cunard.

While the volume of mail and numbers of passengers steadily increased, as did Cunard's competition from the American-flag Ocean Steam Navigation Company, Inman and Collins Line, the size of the original *Britannia* and her sisters was tripled when the twin-funnelled *Persia* of 3,300 tons made her debut in 1856 as the world's then largest passenger steamer. The *Persia* and her later sister the *Scotia*, delivered six years later in 1862, had a unique romantic beauty about them, with the long sleek lines of their hulls and a beautifully balanced profile with their twin funnels located equidistant fore and aft of the paddle-wheel enclosures. Apart from reclaiming the Atlantic Blue Riband honours for speed from their American competitors *Persia* and *Scotia* also brought a vestigial sense of land-based hospitality and reassuring home comfort to the Cunard fleet.

From the sailing packet accommodation approach of Cunard's original *Britannia* and the slightly larger *Cambria* and *Hibernia* that had inaugurated Cunard's direct service between Liverpool and New York in 1848, where a single saloon served as the dining room and gathering place for all other social activity, the *Persia* and *Scotia* brought the added diversity of a library and smoking room. There were two saloons, forward and aft of the machinery spaces and funnels amidships, each with a cupola adding a sense of height and airiness to the interior. There were internal passages on the cabin deck bypassing the machinery spaces amidships, so that passengers could access all parts of the accommodations without having to go by way of the open decks, and for the first time, there was steam heating in the cabins themselves.

Such was the great march of engineering and technological progress that the *Persia* and *Scotia* were at the same time both the last paddle wheelers built for intercontinental service and were pioneer iron-hulled ships. The *Persia* was also a notable pioneer of safety with her hull subdivided into seven watertight compartments and fitted with a double bottom beneath the coal bunkers and cargo holds. Iron soon gave way to steel hull construction and the paddle wheel's prominence was universally usurped by the underwater screw propeller, with the *China* of 1862 being Cunard's first propeller-driven Atlantic liner.[4] These developments changed the appearance and indeed the internal layout of ships, and provided for them to be built in greater sizes with more carrying capacity and higher speeds.

Perhaps of even greater significance is the fact that the mid-1850s-built *Jura* and *Etna* were the first Cunarders to have steerage-class accommodations, which were fitted in 1860.[5] Although the *Jura* and *Etna* were sold the following year, new Cunard passenger ships from 1860 onwards were built with steerage accommodations to serve the growing transatlantic exodus of émigrés to Canada and the United States. The *Russia*, which entered service in 1867 had accommodation for 150 in cabin class and 800 in third or steerage.

The nineteenth century's latter half produced one of the greatest birth booms in history, with the population of England nearly doubling from 16.8 million in 1851 to 30.5 million in 1901.[6] People flocked to the cities in search of employment while the more pastoral ways of life were in decline. Many of those who were fortunate enough to find employment had to live in appalling squalor, with children having to work long hours at menial tasks to help support their families. Furthermore the 1851 census revealed demographic gender imbalance with four percent more women than men, ostensibly contributing to the widespread urban expansion of "The Great Social Evil," as prostitution was then euphemistically referred to by genteel do-gooders. Some 15 million Britons, of both genders and in all walks of life found that their best option was to seek new lives for themselves and their families overseas in Canada, the United States and Australia.

At the same time Cunard's competitors from across the Channel such as Hamburg America Line, North German Lloyd and French Line were, in addition to their own first and cabin trades, likewise conveying

*The **Campania** was already second-generation as a hotel-style Atlantic express liner when she was delivered to Cunard in 1898, being the first to offer single-occupancy cabins and to use the designation "First Class" for the premiere-grade accommodations. (Author's collection)*

Europe's disenchanted and displaced to the New World's more hospitable shores. In 1871 the Liverpool-based White Star Line emerged to become one of Cunard's most formidable competitors, before the two rival Lines were amalgamated during the 1930s. The North Atlantic steamship lines in particular were quick to realise that carrying large numbers of people in basic accommodation with rudimentary service brought an economy of scale that was highly lucrative. About a hundred years later, when the Boeing 747 jumbo jet started to fly, the airline industry was to again discover the good fortunes of mass travel.

The pursuit of prestige and speed continued to flourish, and to form the basis of competition and loyalties for wealthy and influential passengers, though the cost of providing the creature comforts of first and cabin classes and the shortest possible passage times was to some degree underwritten by the great masses crowding the lower decks.

Over the final decades of the Victorian era huge strides were made in shipbuilding and marine engineering, as the paddle wheel gave way, first to the single screw propeller and then to twin screws, and the original side lever engine was replaced by more powerful and fuel-efficient compound multiple-cylinder piston machinery. While Cunard was under contract to the Admiralty for carrying the Royal Mail before this responsibility was transferred to the Postmaster General in 1867, the Line often found itself restricted by Royal Navy's rather conservative approach to innovation in shipbuilding and marine engineering. Advances such as screw propellers and compound engines were only adopted by the Admiralty after very careful evaluation and testing.

15

*The **Lucania**, like the **Campania** had a remarkably clean-lined and modern appearance, for her day as being among the first Cunarders to do away with the auxiliary sailing rig and dispense with the centre mast and its rigging altogether. (Author's collection)*

As the *Persia* was being planned, for instance, the Admiralty had reluctantly agreed to the use of iron for the ship's hull despite having banned its use for mail steamers on the basis of concern for suitability in Naval service if the ship were to be requisitioned as an auxiliary in war time, though they insisted that she be paddle-wheel driven, still believing this to be the more reliable means of propulsion.[7]

Cunard was thus at the competitive disadvantage of being bound to Navy design and building standards in the interest of safeguarding the "swift, regular and safe passage" of Her Majesty's mails. Yet at a time when an ocean crossing was still considered risky, Cunard's outstanding safety record and reputation for regular and punctual service embodied the comfortably secure ideal of swift, safe regular passage, even where their competitors were technologically ahead of them. It is perhaps this point more than anything else that lies behind the mystique of Cunard's tradition that prevails to this day.

The Victorian era's final and greatest triumph of marine engineering was the steam turbine that made possible the building of much larger and faster ships and was the main source of propulsion for ships until well into the latter half of the twentieth century. The turbine's first working prototype was audaciously shown off by its inventor, Charles Algernon Parsons (1854-1931) who virtually stole the show at the 1897 Spithead Naval Review honouring Queen Victoria's Diamond Jubilee by dexterously piloting his own yacht *Turbinia* around the Royal Yacht *Victoria and Albert*, the lines of British and visiting foreign warships and other naval vessels. Built for testing and demonstrating the compact and high-performing steam turbine, the *Turbinia* that day maintained the unprecedented speed of 34.5 knots - too fast even for the Royal Navy patrol boat dispatched to chase her away.[8]

Realising that the navies of other marine powers such as France and Germany would no doubt be swift to adopt this new marvel, the Admiralty was quick to respond. The Royal Navy's first turbine-powered destroyers, the *HMS Cobra* and the *HMS Viper*, were commissioned two years later in 1899. In the twentieth century's opening years, Cunard started planning for the turbine-powered *Lusitania* and *Mauretania*, to be the largest and fastest liners in the world when simultaneously completed in 1907. Cautious as ever, though, the Line first had turbine machinery installed in 1905 aboard the *Carmania*, the second of two otherwise near-identical ships, so that the new machinery's performance could be reliably assessed against the conventionally engined sister ship *Caronia*. Thus, as the Cunard Line came of age, so to speak, at the Victorian era's close in 1901 this final great engineering advance of that epoch set the pace for steam propulsion over the following seventy years.

Hotel at sea

Along with world industrialisation, there came also far greater personal mobility thanks mainly to the railways, the steamship and later the automobile. Although then still to expensive for the great masses, those who could afford it or needed to move about could cover far greater distances in much less time. Travel became a regular necessity of trade and commerce, as raw materials had to be purchased and brought to the manufacturing centres and finished products, including the first consumer goods available to the emerging middle class, were brought to market throughout the land and overseas.

By the late Victorian era, Great Britain and continental Europe were already covered by extensive rail networks, and transcontinental rail services were already operating across North America, Australia and the Indian subcontinent. Steamship service to just about anywhere in the world was regular and reliable, and for those travelling from Britain and Europe to Asia and the Antipodes the voyage was significantly shortened thanks to the Suez Canal. One could travel under steam power, for instance, from central Europe to the Pacific Rim by rail and sea, without having to sail around Cape Horn or cross the Isthmus of Panama, with forward bookings and hotel reservations all being secured ahead of time by telegraph.

With all of this came the first large urban or Grand Hotels, built by the railways as an adjoining part of their city terminus stations, as in the London examples of the Paddington Hotel and St. Pancras Hotel.[9] Like factories and other industrial structures, the railway station and Grand Hotel were a new architectural genre of the age, as the international airport terminal and shopping mall were to develop as new building types of the twentieth century.

As steamships became larger and faster, and inevitably more comfortable, their rival owners began to visualise themselves as much as being in the ocean-going hotel business, at least for first class, as they were purveyors of transport from one place to another.

Hotelism, as it was then called, in effect offered those of the emerging middle class an opportunity for a few days at least, either on dry land or at sea to *live it up* in the style of the wealthy in opulent surroundings, with fine food, beverages and cigars, the companionship of other guests in the public rooms, and an abundance of personal service from obliging staff. For the *filthy rich* it at least maintained the standards they were already accustomed to in their own country homes or townhouses, usually with the added benefit that they could bring along their own valets, butlers and chamber

*The **Aquitania**'s smoking room is shown here in an architectural rendering, giving an impression of the similar decorative opulence of the Cunard headquarters building's executive suites and public areas at Liverpool's Pier Head, also designed at about the same time by Arthur Davis. (Author's collection)*

maids, for whom guest staff accommodation was provided.

Without themselves being the pioneers of significantly higher standards of service and comfort on the North Atlantic, Cunard's *Umbria* and *Etruria* of 1884-5 were nonetheless notable trend setters as veritable sea-going hotels. Following the example of the railway Grand Hotels on *terra firma*, the idea here was to offer the traveller or passenger a sense of celebration of the voyage itself with fine cuisine, accommodation and service at least as good as, if not better than, they could expect at their country estates and private clubs ashore, all within the special milieu of the shipboard life and the by then far more comfortable experience of getting from one place to another.

First and cabin-class passenger accommodations aboard the *Umbria* and *Etruria* were arranged throughout four decks, with walk-around outer promenades at two levels. The first-class public rooms including a spacious dining saloon, used only at meal times, along with a doughnut-shaped music salon on the deck above surrounding a domed central opening through the dining saloon ceiling, a large gentlemen's smoking room, ladies' lounge and boudoir, along with various vestibules and foyers, a barber shop and other services. The ornate furnishing and almost excessive outfitting and decoration of these ships in its reflection of high Victorian affluence rightfully earned them their wide acclaim as "floating hotels."[10]

The twin-propeller *Campania* and *Lucania* of 1893 surpassed ten thousand tons in size at 12,950 tons each, and were the first to be built without auxiliary sailing rig as a backup contingency in case the machinery should fail. Apart from the inevitable refinements to the passenger amenities, which for the first time included

*The **Lusitania**, the Louis XVI First Class dining room's upper level on Shelter Deck with its dome protruding through the accommodations above on the Promenade Deck. (Author's collection)*

deckchair rental and cabins for single travellers, the interior decoration was of acknowledged Elizabethan, Italian Renaissance and other period styles.[11]

When the *Lusitania* and *Mauretania*, followed in 1907 as Cunard's first two true *superliners*, period styling of the first- and cabin-class passenger interiors had already set a comfortable traditionalist standard for the Line's shipboard architecture. It was elegant and entirely liveable, rendered in an entirely human scale without being outsized, ostentatious or overpowering. The style reflected values that passengers would be at home and familiar with through its similarity with the design of hotels ashore such as the new Ritz Hotels in Paris and London, The Dorchester or New York's Waldorf Astoria. This was also the style of upper-class establishments such as The Athenian and Royal Automobile Club and the executive offices of financial, commercial and industrial enterprises on both sides of the Atlantic.

Publicity literature, books and magazines of the day often referred to interior decoration of this type, either ashore or afloat, as being *typical* of a "stately British country home."[12] Those elements or artefacts of Elizabethan, Italian Renaissance or Louis XVI still to be found in the gentry's country houses existed still from those times when the houses were either built or extensively modified and reflected the whim and fancy of their owners, recalling perhaps their travels abroad. The art of institutional period revival that was reaching its zenith in the twentieth century's opening years was scholarly design work carefully devised to assert an atmosphere of *bon vivant* in the commercially motivated surroundings of ships, hotels or private clubs. It was never to convey any theme or notion that was too profound or severe, but rather to assert a pleasing background of classical flourishes and whimsy for the enjoyment of modern twentieth century living without being reminded of anything too lofty or serious.

With the greater size and complexity of the *Lusitania* and *Mauretania* and the added design sophistication of their passenger accommodations, Cunard engaged professional architects for the first time to co-ordinate the design and decoration of the first-class public spaces along with the deluxe cabins and suites. James Miller (1860-1947,), whose experience included hotels, public buildings, rail and underground stations in the west of Scotland, was commissioned for the *Lusitania*[13] and prominent London residential architect Harold A. Peto (1854-1933) for the *Mauretania*.[14] Although neither had any ship design experience, nor had hotel design by then emerged as a specialty, the results they achieved were truly outstanding.

While the two ships were nearly identical in structure, engineering and layout, the interior architecture and decoration of each was unique. Peto's work aboard the

19

*The **Lusitania**, seen here in an un-captioned photograph, probably taken at Liverpool early in her short career. (Author's collection)*

Mauretania drew mainly on historic French influences, as the choice of these ashore had become fashionable in upper-class circles on both sides of the Atlantic, reflecting an apparent understanding of French interior decorating styles among the wealthy and well educated. The ship's double-height domed main dining room was decorated in a sixteenth-century François I style panelled in dark Austrian oak and the main lounge in a Louis XVI style with mahogany panelling and marble columns. Miller's Louis XVI *Lusitania* dining room used enamelled white panelling with gilded detailing and a Georgian style prevailed throughout her main suite of public rooms. The differing decorative schemes served best for passengers to distinguish one ship from the other as other differing structural detail in the superstructure fronts and ventilator cowls were probably too esoteric to be noticed by most passengers.

The *Lusitania* and *Mauretania* handily achieved their competitive objective of wresting the Blue Riband honours from North German Lloyd's *Deutschland* of 1899, only to face a different sort of challenge, mainly from Hamburg America and White Star, which were stressing higher standards of hotel luxury and service rather than speed records. White Star's *Olympic*, and Hamburg America's *Imperator* delivered in 1911 and 1913 were both very large ships for the time with high superstructures housing large numbers of luxury rooms and suites and extensive suites of opulent public rooms surrounded by glass-enclosed promenades. Cunard responded with the 45,647-ton *Aquitania* completed shortly before the outbreak of World War I in 1914.

Design of the *Aquitania*'s interiors was co-ordinated by the Parisian hotel architect Charles Mevès (1860-1914) by then noted for his designs of the Paris and London Ritz Hotels and his English partner Arthur Davis (1878-1951), Mevès and Davis had already designed the Ritz style first class interiors for Hamburg America Line's *Amerika* of 1905, and Mevès had since been commissioned for the interiors of the *Imperator* and *Vaterland* to be handled by a German collaborator, Alphonse Bischoff through his own practice in Cologne. By this arrangement Mevès could in effect work with the two competing steamship lines so long as there was no direct exchange of details between Davis and Boscoff or through Mevès. Cunard had in fact approached Mevès and Davis in 1905 to design interiors for the *Lusitania* and *Mauretania*, though at the time they were already committed to their *Amerika* commission.

Widely known as *The ship beautiful*,[15] Cunard's *Aquitania* was probably the finest period revivalist work done by Mevès and Davis, and certainly their last as Charles Mevès himself died the same year as her delivery. The various period styles used throughout the *Aquitania*'s public rooms were in many instances based on specific places ashore, with the smoking room, for instance, being adapted from a Charles II-period hall at Greenwich Hospital, and the main lounge modelled after the work of Sir Christopher Wren, reflecting his use of classic columns and entablature, and preference for classic white wall surfaces. A Brothers Adam style was chosen for the drawing room, domed deck entrance and reception room and long gallery. The writing room and an elegat ladies' lounge were in Louis XVI style. These and numerous other styles were used for the first-class cabins and suites.

As delightfully *old world* as this was, it nonetheless reflected the best in modern hotel architecture at the time. The *Aquitania* was herself an otherwise entirely modern ship, with entirely contemporary standards of hotel comfort and service. The cabins in particular reflected a standard at par with the best hotels on land, featuring large rectangular rooms with full-sized bedsteads and many of these having separate en-suite bathrooms and lavatories. For Cunard, the *Aquitania* probably best represented the values of traditional hospitality and service and the notion of "swift, regular and safe passage" upon which the Line and its enviable reputation was built. In the decades to follow, it would seem that perhaps the *Aquitania* embodied a *personality* that Cunard was reluctant to compromise to the whims of architectural and design *modernists* or perhaps also even to changing lifestyles.

Flirting with *moderne*

Even before the outbreak of World War I in August 1914, Hamburg America Line that year showed at the Werkbund Exhibition[16] in Cologne mock-up ship interiors of a simpler neo-classical style intended to set a new design direction for the Line's ships. The same exhibition also featured railway sleeper compartments and dining cars kitchen and serving facilities that were to greatly influence apartment design in the post-war age, with compact plans making wide use of built-in fixtures and furnishings.[17] In light of these developments and their inevitable influences also on ship design, Victorian era revivalist styles with their excessive artistic flourishes and curlicues were already becoming passé.

Another exhibition eleven years later, this one the *Exposition Internationale des Arts Industrielles et Décoratifs* which ran through the summer of 1925 in post-World War I Paris, served to assert the great influences of modern twentieth-century design and art throughout the Western World. The French Line's new transatlantic liner *Ile de France* in effect brought the *Exposition* to New York on her maiden voyage two years later through her stunningly modern interior and decorative design. The ship was a veritable showcase of French *moderne* created by many of the same people whose work had featured prominently at the *Exposition*. These featured modern indirect and concealed lighting and an abundant use of mirrored glass, glossy veneers and bright metallic surfaces with soft furnishings in bold saturated colours and a great wealth of contemporary French art.

The *Ile de France* was followed by other ships reflecting the modern architecture and design of other nations, including Sweden's *Kungsholm* of 1928, Germany's rakish record-breaking *Bremen* and *Europa* at the end of the

*The **Aquitania** alongside at Southampton Docks during the inter War years. (Author's collection)*

decade and Italy's fashionably modern 1932 *Conte di Savoia*. The ultimate expression of this genre was French Line's magnificent *Normandie* completed in 1935 as the first of the liner era's three great 80,000-ton superships. Decoratively, the *Normandie* was a sophisticated refinement of the *Ile de France*, rendered by many of the same designers, yet arranged on an axial plan that offered broad vistas through a remarkable series of open plan public rooms of double height.

Cunard, whose own superliner the *Queen Mary* was due to make her debut in 1936, had in the meantime kept up its own express North Atlantic service with the *Mauretania* and *Aquitania* and *Berengaria*, the former *Imperator* acquired in reparation for the *Lusitania*'s loss during World War I. While these ships had all undergone extensive modernisation refits, including conversion from coal to oil firing of their boilers and substantial upgrading of their cabin accommodations, mainly to provide greater numbers of cabins with en-suite toilets and baths, the *Mauretania*'s Harold Peto public interiors and those of Mevès and Davis aboard the *Aquitania* and *Berengaria* remained largely unaltered as the Line's enduring house style.

While it would seem that Cunard itself, along with its regular clientele were happy enough with the design status quo and content to leave *moderne* to the Europeans, concern was expressed within design circles as to whether the new then still unnamed Cunard superliner could be expected to portray a more appropriately contemporary impression of British design progress.

An illustrated editorial feature in the prestigious professional periodical *The Architects' Journal* pointed out that while hospitality ashore had generally progressed to a far more contemporary style of, for instance, the fashionable new Morecomb Hotel, the British liner was still caught in a time warp of "the dear old Waldorf." It went to ask that if the new Cunard was to have one of those names from the old Roman Provinces ending in "ia," could it at least please be something closer to *Contemporania* that we may be seen abroad as being something more than merely "a nation of olde-worlde shopkeepers?"[18]

Arthur Davis was commissioned to co-ordinate the interior design of hull number 534 that was to be launched as the *Queen Mary* in league with New York architect Benjamin Wistar Morris to advise on American style and taste. Like Davis, Morris's background was in the Beaux Arts style, and his work ashore had included Cunard's Manhattan offices, designed in a similar style to Mevès and Davis's work on the Line's headquarters at Liverpool's Pier head, dating from 1916. The *Queen Mary*'s structural design and internal layout was fairly conventional, drawing upon the proven success of ships such as *Aquitania*. The architectural design and decoration was drawn from contemporary British and American influences that reflected the times of its creation, but inevitably lacked *Normandie*'s Gallic panache and *grande gesture*. While this came as something of a disappointment to some, it was nonetheless consistent with Cunard's own traditional ideals of "swift, regular and safe passage" in the luxury of the world's biggest liner and ultimately proved to be commercially successful.

The *Queen Elizabeth* completed four years later in 1940 and only inaugurated in transatlantic passenger service after the end of World War II was similar in overall design concept, outfitting and interior decoration. Structurally she was, however, considerably more modern, with two, rather than three, funnels and with the ventilation intakes concentrated around the bases of these, as was done with the *Normandie*, resulting in a likewise more straightforward layout of her public rooms with greater openness of plan. Benjamin Morris was again engaged to handle the interior design, this time working with George Grey Wornum as his British counterpart. Wornum was noted for his design of the Royal Incorporation of British Architects (RIBA) headquarters in Portland Place in London. The *Queen Elizabeth*'s interiors were a little less eclectic than those of the earlier ship, showing a higher degree of architectural *correctness* akin to the RIBA building.

Until planning was started in the mid 1950s for ships that would eventually replace the *Queens*, a number of smaller intermediate-class liners were built for service on Cunard's Canadian route to Montréal, reflecting a post World War II trend towards smaller ships with greater emphasis on tourist-class accommodations to meet the needs of that era's emigration boom. The interiors of these were designed in an eclectic style described by the

Line as "recreating the past in terms of the present by using modern methods of construction." It was a somewhat *overdressed* style that seemed to be focused on reminiscences of a *past* that never really ever existed – it disappeared by the mid 1960s when two of the ships were redecorated in a more genuinely contemporary mode for cruising and the others were sold.

Meanwhile the *Queens* virtually became 1930s revivalist pieces in their own time as their interior architecture aged gracefully into settings reminiscent of a bygone era in grand-luxe travel when great ocean liners catered to Hollywood film stars, sports celebrities, business tycoons and even heads of state, most of who had since taken to air travel. Famed also for their War service, these great and grand old ships became veritable institutions that upheld, especially for Americans, the romantic traditional notion of Britain and all things British. For Britons this also upheld a special cultural relationship with ships and the sea, stressing the more traditional maritime milieu of veneer panelled interiors with leather upholstered smoking room club chairs and teak-planked open decks where one could still promenade and breath the sea air. The effect of all these factors was then heightened all the more by its stark contrast with the modernity of leading foreign post-war ships such America's final Blue Riband champion *United States*, Holland America's elegant new *Rotterdam* and the 1950s haut moderne of the French Line's elite *France*.

Yet in the 1960s, when Cunard was planning for the ship that would eventually be launched as the *Queen Elizabeth 2*, Britain and things British had suddenly become hip, cool and *mod* as the nation was swept by a revolution in pop that took the whole Western World by storm. There was a remarkable universality in the catchy upbeat music of Sixties rock bands such as the Beatles and Rolling Stones, and in the bright, simple and affordable fashions of the day such as the Mary Quant mini skirt and Barbara Hulanicki's flowing biba styles that appealed to all ages, nationalities and classes and was as at home in Britain's suburban new towns such as Stevenage, Basildon and Hemel Hempstead, as it was in London, New York, Paris or Milan.

Cunard too became caught up in the tempo of the times, as the *QE2* was to emerge as a veritable icon of twentieth century British modernity at its absolute best. It had taken lobbying on the part of the architectural and industrial design professions, with questions even being asked in Parliament as to why what was to become Britain's merchant flagship should represent anything less than the Nation's absolute best in her design and artistic decoration. As had been done with the old *Queens*, the new ship was being built with Crown loan guarantees and thus entitling the state and ultimately the taxpayers to have their say in the matter. With the Design Council's help a design team was put together for the new Cunarder that included prominent people who were progressive and forward looking though without being too radical. Their modernist approach to realising this commission would reference the social and technological progress of the jet and space age, with new materials and aesthetics of the times.[19]

The team was headed by James Gardner (1907-95), responsible for the ship's exterior design and styling and Dennis Lennon (1919-91) heading a carefully selected cadre of prominent architects and designers who would create her myriad public interiors, suites and cabins. These included Professor Misha Black (1910-77) and Sir Hugh Casson (1910-99) who had previously worked with Gardner on designing the pavilions, structures and exhibits for the 1951 Festival of Britain exhibition and

*The **Queen Mary** seen here during the 1960s at her home berth in Southampton Docks alongside the old Ocean Terminal. (John Hendy)*

had also done modern ship interiors for P&O Orient Lines.

At the time of her debut in the spring of 1969 the *QE2* provided a substantial glimpse into the future of luxury worldwide cruising. Apart from her stunningly attractive modern exterior lines and crisply contemporary interiors, the ship herself was in fact designed primarily for cruising without class barriers with her alternative role in transatlantic service for two loosely segregated classes of service being secondary.[20] As far as possible passenger accommodations were pushed outwards towards the sides of the ship to reduce the number of inside cabins to the barest minimum and to concentrate the public rooms, including the restaurants on the uppermost decks where these would have the greatest exposure to natural light and direct access to

the outer decks. Sir Hugh Casson described the ship as being "an hotel on its head: four decks of public rooms of great variety of size and character, above five decks of bedrooms."[21]

Among the ship's most outstanding public spaces were the Queen's Room, with its backlit latticed ceiling and elegant trumpet-shaped columns and bold wood-block wall panelling, the Double Room designed around a double-deck central space with a wide sweeping curved staircase joining its upper and lower levels and the circular main entrance foyer panelled in dark smoky veneers beneath a serrated fibreglass ceiling devised to create the impressions of the concentric ripples created by dropping a stone into a pond. The cabins and suites had more the look of modern hotel rooms, close carpeted throughout and all with their own en-suite toilets.

The shipbuilding journal *Shipbuilding and Shipping Record* hailed *QE2* as "A ship with a past and a future," looking back to Cunard's then nearly 130 years of liner experience and forward to the dawning of a new era in luxury worldwide cruising – with the *QE2* the Line almost immediately became a leader and innovator in cruise ships. Indeed deluxe cruise ships such as the *Sea Venture* and *Royal Viking Star* clearly showed the *QE2*'s direct influence in their design.

On board with Carnival

In 1998 Cunard became part of, and indeed was in effect rescued by, the Carnival Group. In the nearly three decades that had passed since the *QE2*'s debut, the Line had only taken delivery of two pairs of much smaller purpose-built new cruise ships in the 1970s and had subsequently acquired the former Norwegian America Line *Sagafjord* and *Vistafjord* as more suitable smaller running mates for *QE2* in luxury world-side

*The **Queen Elizabeth**, seen here in Lower Swinging Ground at Southampton Docks, shows a slightly more modern profile than the **Queen Mary**, with twin freestanding funnels and no forward well deck. (John Hendy)*

*The **Caronia** completed in 1949, with her distinctive pea green hull colour, was a smaller luxury rendition of the Queens, capable of North Atlantic service, though intended primarily for cruising. (John Hendy)*

cruising, with the *Vistafjord* later being renamed *Caronia*. Meanwhile, Carnival Cruises and other pioneers of modern-era cruising such as Royal Caribbean, Norwegian Caribbean, along with Cunard's old liner-era companions Costa, Holland America and P&O were aggressively building ever larger fleets of spectacular new cruise ships.

Since 1971, Cunard had been owned by Trafalgar House, a large and diverse British conglomerate, which otherwise had no particular focus on shipping and shipbuilding. During this period the *QE2* went through numerous refits, refurbishments, reconfigurations, as well as a complete re-engining in 1986-7, all aimed at retaining her position of great prestige against ever increasing competition. More and more the public's

perception of Cunard was becoming that it primarily supported the *QE2* as its one and only ship in the size league of its competition, with the *Sagafjord* and *Vistafjord* / *Caronia* being viewed as but lesser secondary fleet mates despite the high standard of their accommodation and service. A new *Queen* code-named *Q5* was proposed during the 1990s but was still on the drawing board by the time Carnival acquired Cunard.

Plans needed to be laid for the gracefully aging *QE2*'s eventual replacement with a new cruise-oriented North Atlantic liner. Fleet mates of similar size and comparable prestige would also be needed to further develop and expand the unique Cunard *product* on the same basis as other cruise brands of a similarly traditional origin such as Costa, Holland America and P&O. With the immense

*The **Queen Elizabeth 2** is seen here high atop the inclined launching ways at a fairly advanced stage of building in the summer of 1967 shortly before her launching. (Bruce Peter collection)*

popularity and devoted regular following of the *QE2* as probably the world's best-known and most-loved liner of all times the Cunard brand was sure to be a sound bet for Carnival. For Cunard, there was the great advantage of being adopted by a new corporate parent with the resources to build on the grand scale needed to bring its long and illustrious history into a third century of its existence.

Carnival itself traces its own origins to a rather shaky start in 1972 as a one-ship operation when Canadian Pacific's redundant *Empress of Canada* was purchased for a knock-down price, deadheaded to Miami and hurriedly put into cruise service *as is*. Legend has it that there was only enough paint on board to partly cover

the Canadian Pacific *multimark* funnel insignia, turning it into a stylised letter C that has remained ever since as the Carnival logo. Meanwhile, tickets for a short introductory cruise to Puerto Rico were being sold on Miami Beach for as little as ten dollars apiece. Renamed *Mardi Gras*, the ship suffered the unfortunate embarrassment of grounding on a sandbar in the Government Cut on her way out to sea from the Port of Miami's Dodge Island pier, though fortunately she was later re-floated undamaged. The preview cruise was ultimately a success and set the pace for Carnival's initial success in inexpensive and informal mass-market Caribbean cruising.

Two additional liners were acquired during the 1970s,

*The **Queen Elizabeth 2**'s modern Double Room was originally fitted with a wide semi-circular staircase that was a key focal point of the room opposite its bandstand. (Bruce Peter collection)*

including the Greek Line *Queen Anna Maria*, originally Canadian Pacific's *Empress of Britain* of 1956 and Safmarine's *SA Vaal*, delivered in 1961 to Union Castle Line as the *Transvaal Castle*. Musicians from the original *Empress of Canada* ship's orchestra who had signed on with Carnival recalled that this had always been a very happy ship both for passengers and crew, inspiring the new owners to change their branding idea from "The Golden Fleet" to "The Fun Ships," a name that aptly defined Carnival's core product, its development and identity for many years to come.

In 1980 Carnival's Danish-built *Tropicale* was the first in a spate of new cruise ships in the then large over-30,000-ton range, followed almost immediately by the more upscale Home Lines *Atlantic*, HAPAG-Lloyd *Europa* and Holland America *Nieuw Amsterdam* and *Noordam*. Compared with these, *Tropicale* made a far less traditional impression with her rakish lines, big gull-winged funnel, somewhat resembling the tail of a Boeing

727 airliner and her crooked row of cascading porthole-style windows following the gradual slope of the show-lounge floor inside, all of which were to become trademark Carnival features. The *Tropicale* was followed mid decade by the 45,000-ton *Holiday* and her two slightly larger sister ships *Celebration* and *Jubilee* from the Cockums yard in Sweden. Through the 1990s the Carnival fleet grew exponentially with the addition of eight Finnish-built 70,000-ton ships in the *Fantasy* series.

With the great success of its own brand, Carnival was looking to diversify into the more upscale league of other lines such as Holland America, Princess Cruises and Royal Viking Line. While the company's Project Tiffany was aimed at expanding into this market sector under a new brand of its own, the decision was finally made to instead absorb an upscale cruise line with an already established product and existing clientele, with Holland America Line being acquired by Carnival in 1989. Holland America was to retain its own name and

*The **Queen Elizabeth 2**'s Columbia Restaurant was entered from a raised podium incorporated into the midships stairway enabling passengers to make a grand descent to their tables at mealtimes. (Miles Cowsill)*

*The **Queen Elizabeth 2** raises steam for her maiden-voyage sailing from Southampton's Ocean Terminal on Friday, 2nd May 1969. (Bruce Peter collection)*

much of its unique character and national identity, while at the same time fulfilling Carnival's objective of diversifying into the upscale cruise market and benefiting from the vast technical resources and extensive shipbuilding activity of its new owners.

Existing plans for two new Holland American ships were scrapped, with the *Statendam*, designed and built under the direction of Carnival's own technical department and delivered three years later in 1992. With luxury accommodation for 1,266 passengers in lower berths only and a measure of 55,000 tons, she was the first in a series of four ships, followed by the slightly larger *Rotterdam* and two additional ships in her league towards the decade's end.

With Cunard's 1998 acquisition, Carnival had absorbed probably the most prestigious name in the passenger shipping and cruise industry. Even though by then the *QE2*'s accommodations and amenities were in some regards no longer state-of-the-art, the aura of her unique singularity and the traditions behind her existence held tremendous trading value and public appeal. What needed to be done was to sustain these values through new generations of ships that would ultimately replace the world renowned and much-loved existing flagship.

Already named *Queen Mary 2* at an early stage of her planning, the new Cunard transatlantic liner was the only ship to be planned and built under Carnival's direction as a unique one-of-a-kind entity since *Tropicale* was delivered some two decades earlier. As Cunard's first large new liner since the *QE2* she was also to introduce a quantum change in design approach, with the introduction of post-*QE2* features such as a predominance of veranda cabin accommodations on the upper decks for the first time aboard a vessel designed to withstand the rigours of continuous express service on the North Atlantic. In view of the added height of the hull's sides needed for North Atlantic service, the cabins and suites were arranged above and below a secondary central run of public rooms atop the hull, with the three strata of accommodations below having verandas protected behind openings in the hull's sides. The main suite of public spaces below these, including a spectacular triple-height main restaurant and a fully functional planetarium with a retractable projection dome, was laid out on a grand scale following a grand central promenade plan inspired by the *Normandie*.

Architecturally, the new ship showed little of the *QE2*'s original crisp clean-lined modernity, which bit by bit had by then been gradually whittled away from the older ship through the many refits and other changes made over the years. Some rooms had been changed completely, such as the original 736 Club discotheque and bar that had become the Queen's Grill restaurant, while others such as the elegant Look Out lounge forward on Upper Deck had disappeared altogether, and the Double Room had been revamped numerous times in an effort to make it into a cabaret lounge, a purpose for which its space was never ever intended.

Because of the *QE2*'s great popularity and devoted following of regular passengers who would ultimately want to sail aboard the new ship, there was the feeling that some of her features such as the Queen's Room and the Golden Lion Pub, itself the product of a mid 1990s refit, should be brought forward at least in spirit even without the ship's original modernity. The design approach developed for the new *Queen Mary 2* also had to avoid being so different as to be difficult to be adapted to later cruise ships that would inevitably be built for the Line.

31

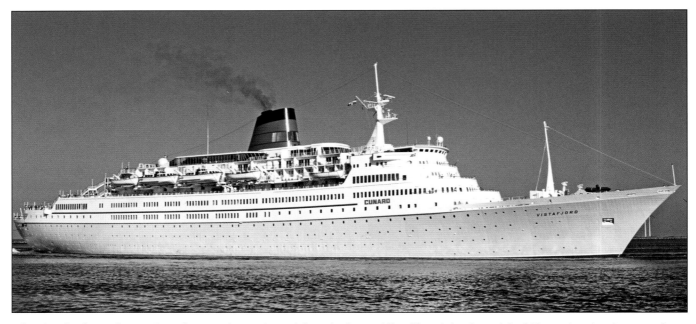

*The **Vistafjord**, seen here at Copenhagen, takes on Cunard funnel colours while still retaining her original Norwegian America name for Cunard's European-based cruise services. (Bruce Peter)*

The *Queen Mary 2* was completed and handed over to Cunard in late 2003 as the then largest passenger ship in the world at 148,250 tons and with a lower-berth passenger capacity of 2,620 persons. Her unique hull was designed with the great structural strength and added freeboard height above the waterline height needed for Atlantic crossings and other long sea passages at a relatively high service speed of 28.5 knots. This was achieved without compromise to the high proportion of outer and veranda cabins expected by passengers or to the wide range of deck facilities expected for cruising in temperate and tropical waters, and with the addition of a number of significant amenities and design features that would set the *QM2* apart as a truly singular ship.

By the time of Cunard's acquisition, Carnival's

technical department and shipbuilding activities were organised as an entity called Carnival Corporate Shipbuilding, as a sort of one-stop service for the fleet development activities of the Corporation's various subsidiaries. By then these also included Costa Cruises which joined the Group in the year 2000 as part of an expansion into the European cruise market. Following the success of long *Fantasy* and *Statendam* series-building programmes for the Carnival and Holland America fleets, the next generation of ships was planned so that each new series would be readily adaptable to the individual characteristics of more than one subsidiary within the group.

In essence this meant the overall hull form, structural configuration and layout, along with machinery and other technical installations, stores and baggage handling, food and beverages, hotel and housekeeping services, and crew facilities would be identical and operationally interchangeable. This would form an underlying platform around which the exterior styling, accommodation and arrangement of passenger facilities, along with their interior architecture and styling would be tailored to the specific needs and tastes, first of the subsidiary's fleet and product identity and then of each ship herself, preserving the individuality of character and identity for which most people find ships to be so irresistibly interesting.

This approach was applied with the *Spirit* series of four large standard-market ships built in Finland, of which she and the *Costa Atlantica* and the *Carnival Spirit* were the first to be delivered in the years 2000 and 2001 respectively. In all, six 2,142-passenger 85,820-ton ships were built in this series of which four went to Carnival and two to Costa. These were designed to a new Panamax-max standard with maximum dimensions allowing them the flexibility to squeeze through the Panama Canal.

Meanwhile, Carnival's more upscale *Vista Class* made its first appearance in 2002 as Holland America's 81,769-ton *Zuiderdam*, with spacious luxury accommodations for 1,848 passengers in lower berths. Quite significantly, this ship was also aimed at attracting a younger clientele to luxury cruising, with a greater range of public facilities in lighter and brighter colours, reflecting more choice but still keeping the established Holland America sense of intimacy and sense of luxury. The Dutch firm VFD Interiors, which had handled the interior design of the Line's ships since the *Nieuw Amsterdam* and *Noordam* in the early 1980s was again commissioned for the new *Vista* ships.

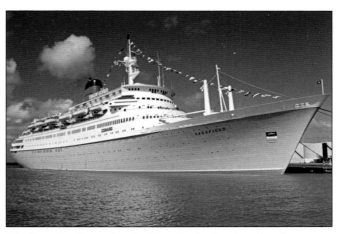

*The **Sagafjord** served as the **Vistafjord**'s American-based counterpart under the Cunard house flag. (Bruce Peter)*

Initially, five ships were ordered in the series for completion between 2002 and 2005, of which the fourth was originally earmarked to go to Cunard as a first fleet mate for the *Queen Mary 2*. This allocation was made well before the *QM2*'s completion at a time when contracts had already been signed for the *Vista* ship's interior design and outfitting, and steel, machinery and other major items already ordered for her building. It was eventually decided that more time was needed to tailor the new ship to Cunard's own style of service and other specific requirements, as well as to have time to assess the *QM2*'s performance in service and to determine which of her features would win the greatest public appeal and be most suitable for adaptation to the new Cunard ship.

The fourth *Vista* ship was allocated instead to P&O Cruises, which had then just come into the fold through a 2003 merger of Carnival Corporation and P&O Princess Cruises, and was completed in 2005 as the *Arcadia*. She differed outwardly from the earlier Holland

America ships of her class by way of a glass-sided pod atop the superstructure, housing various public spaces added around the funnel's base. This is in fact serves to contain a convergence of the forward and aft engine uptakes to the twin funnels of the Holland America ships for the single funnels of this and the later Cunard ship where similar structures are also added. The *Arcadia* is the only *Vista* to have a white hull, itself alone distinguishing her perhaps more than anything else from the others.

From the outset this ship's public interiors were to have reflected a more modern design approach,

reflecting some of the more contemporary elements of the *QM2*, done by the London-based designteam, which had worked with SMC and Sweden's Tillberg Design on the *QM2*. This is perhaps best realised in the triple-height elliptical lobby atrium's stark elegance. While the *Arcadia* shows a high standard of architectural design, the asymmetrical layout of her public rooms, still reflects Holland America preferences, indicating that indeed more time would have been needed to realise a plan more specifically suited to Cunard's expectations.

A sixth *Vista* ship, 11.36 metres longer at the water line, and with additional hull strengthening of the bow

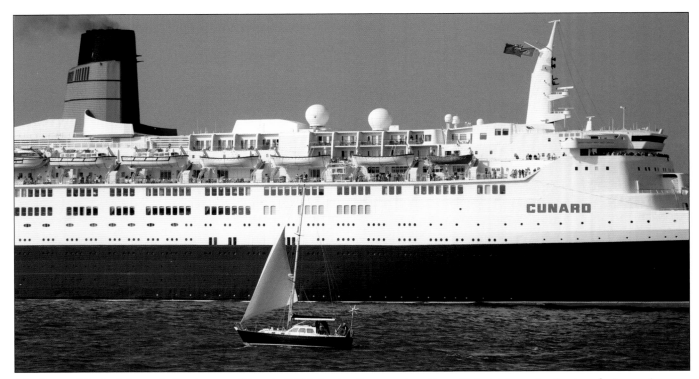

*The **Queen Elizabeth 2** seen in Southampton Water in 2008 showing the veranda cabins added atop her superstructure during various refits and refurbishments done during her career as well as the larger funnel from her Diesel-refit. (Miles Cowsill)*

*The **Arcadia**, originally earmarked to become Cunard's **Queen Victoria**, was completed for P&O as the only Vista-class ship thus far to have a white hull. (Miles Cowsill)*

and forward superstructure for occasional transatlantic crossings and other long ocean passages, was ordered for completion as Cunard's *Queen Victoria* at the end of 2007. As part of a two-billion-dollar deal with the Italian Fincantieri shipbuilding group, this was ordered along with an additional *Vista* ship for Holland America, completed in 2008 as *Eurodam*, with an option for one additional sister, as well as one each for Princess Cruises' in the 116,000-ton *Grand Princess* series and a new larger 130,000 version of the *Carnival Destiny* series, eclipsing the already larger *Carnival Conquest* series measure of 110,239 tons and greater length of 290 metres. These were delivered respectively as Holland America's *Eurodam*, *Emerald Princess* and *Carnival Dream* in 2007 and 2009 respectively.[22] The options were taken up as *Ruby Princess* in 2008 and *Nieuw Amsterdam* to come into service later in 2010.

With added time available for planning and design, Cunard was able to pursue an approach with greater emphasis on the Line's rich history and tradition. The name *Queen Victoria* makes a connection with the Victorian era during which the Cunard Line was born and flourished through a period of great growth and development, and which continues to this day to be identified with the Line's rich history and traditions. The *Queen Victoria* was originally favoured for Cunard's first *Queen* liner in the 1930s, as it fitted the Line's convention of naming its passenger ships after old Roman provinces ending with the letters *ia*. Legend has it though that when King George V was asked for his consent to naming the new Cunarder for "Britain's greatest Queen," apparently replied that his wife would be delighted with that, and the ship ended up accordingly being launched as the *Queen Mary*.

Where *Heritage Trails* had been worked into the *QE2*'s extensive Project Lifestyle refit in the mid 1990s and included in the decoration of the *QM2* as permanent exhibitions of various historical artefacts and memorabilia, the new ship's architecture would itself make the connection with direct references to the liner era. This would be emphasised with greater recourse to double and triple-height public spaces of the old *Queens*, and of the second *Mauretania* and the distinctive 1949-built *Caronia* that captured the travelling public's imagination during the early post World War II period, before the luxury trade started taking to the jet airways in the late 1950s. Yet the new ship's design leitmotif would also look farther back from this era to the earlier influences of *Aquitania*, the Ship Beautiful, to the first *Mauretania*, and beyond to other relevant historical influences on land as well as at sea. The idea was that rather than trying to copy these influences they should be adapted as a sort of theatrical setting or scenography for their enjoyment within the context of twenty-first century luxury travel and living in settings that are evocative of the liner era and the age of grand-luxe travel and hospitality.

Other changes from the original *Vista*-series plan, developed for primarily American-based cruising, would reflect a more British approach to the lifestyle amenities offered, with for instance, greater emphasis on ballroom dancing and the style of entertainment and leisure activities preferred by Britons at sea. With the ship being built and financed entirely by private enterprise, there would be no questions asked about the choices of interior design schemes in Parliament and no recommendations offered by the Design Council or the architectural and interior design professions, with Cunard and Carnival and their partners being left entirely free to make their own choices for the type of ship they really wanted to have.

If Cunard had wanted a new corporate parent or sponsor willing to invest in the large-scale fleet redevelopment programme they needed to remain competitive in twenty-first century upscale cruising they could have done no better than to be a part of Carnival Corporation and a client of Carnival Corporate Shipbuilding's extensive sphere of activity.

*The **Queen Victoria** arrives in the morning light at Southampton. (Andrew Cooke)*

CHAPTER 2

DESIGNING AND BUILDING THE QUEEN VICTORIA

CUNARD

QUEEN VICTORIA

Much of what is done in the art of designing and building ships, even those of the greatest prestige and highest degree of luxury, is by *reference* to other vessels that are already built, are proven in service and of specific interest to the owners and operators. Part of the early planning work involves identifying specific *reference ships* upon which is rooted just about anything from the overall dimensions and hull form, speed and carrying capacity, through choices of propulsion machinery, auxiliary systems and various technical and behind the scenes services to the layout of passenger spaces, and in particular the details of the cabins and suites and all that their outfitting and equipping entails. The ultimate success of this approach lies in the degree of success with which the influence of reference ships is shaped and tailored to assert a unique character and identity for the new ship.

In a series building scheme such as the *Vista* upon which the *Queen Victoria* is based, the overall enclosing *envelope* of hull and superstructure are for the most part already quite literally cast in steel. Some overall lengthening of the hull is possible, as was done for the *Queen Victoria*. There is also a degree of flexibility to alter various details of the superstructure mass and configuration, the funnels and other structures without changing the shipyard tooling and fabrication processes already in place for the series as a whole.

Vista already offered the sort of solid deep-sea liner stance Cunard needed for the *Queen Victoria*, by virtue of the size and structural stamina needed for Holland America's worldwide cruising programmes. The freeboard height of the hull's sides from the waterline to the open promenade beneath the lifeboats encloses a full four decks behind solid steel plating, with openings only for windows and a few access hatches. This is one deck

*The **Queen Victoria**'s first hull block is suspended from a gantry crane above the building dock awaiting its ceremonial lowering as the modern equivalent of the traditional keel laying. (Fincantieri)*

higher than for some other ships of similar size designed for service over shorter distances in predominantly tropical waters. The dark colour of this in both the Holland America ships and *Queen Victoria* also conveys more the visual expression of a deep-sea liner than of a tropical ship. Forward of the lifeboats, the hull's solid shell plating is carried upwards to the deck above and extended completely around the bow mooring deck, adding to the classic liner look of greater height and structural strength.

The liner profile, and indeed performance at sea, of the *Queen Victoria* also benefits from the added 11.36 metres of her overall length. As is usually done when *stretching* in a series building, the greater length of the *Queen Victoria* is gained by inserting an additional block in the centre-body of the hull, in much the same way that the aviation industry inserts a fuselage *plug* ahead of the wing spar to gain the added carrying capacity in the *stretched* variant of a particular aircraft type. The *Queen*

Top pictures: Two views of the **Queen Victoria** *in her final stages of construction. (Pascal Baetens)*

Above: The **Queen Victoria** *receives her aft-most section of the double bottom with the propulsion pod emplacements lowered into position. (Fincantieri)*

Right: The **Queen Victoria**'s *structural assembly nears completion as the entire Commodore Club enclosure is lifted atop the navigating bridge. (Fincantieri)*

Victoria's added section, which corresponds exactly to the combined 2.8-metre widths of four standard cabins is in fact inserted just ahead of the forward machinery space and the engine control room, approximately where the outer panoramic lifts are located in the original Holland American *Vista* ships.

The *Queen Victoria*'s added section is difficult to identify by sight, thanks to an overall smoothing out of her exterior lines, with the panoramic outward-facing lifts of the Holland America ships being replaced by an internal lift- and stair-tower at the ship's centre line to achieve greater flexibility in the layout of larger deluxe cabins and suites on the accommodation decks. The upper accommodation decks were extended farther astern, shortening the afterdecks terracing to also increase the overall amount of internal accommodation space. The overall aesthetic effect of these changes was to strengthen the horizontal visual impact of the ship's form as an ocean liner. As such, the *Queen Victoria*, with her distinctive big stocky *QE2* diesel-era-style Cunard funnel, and other unique features is arguably the most attractive of the *Vista* ships and a worthy and compatible fleet mate for the *Queen Mary 2*.

Internally, the *Queen Victoria* differs from her *Vista* and *Signature* counterparts mainly in the layout and style of her public rooms. While the catering facilities and other services retain the same location and extent as aboard the Holland America ships, the public spaces on Decks 2 and 3 otherwise follow a more direct and open plan, with generally larger spaces, and a number of these extending through the full height of both decks. The open promenade surrounding these is improved, with more space for strolling and for traditional wood-frame deckchairs with comfortable cushions and pillows thanks to space-saving refinements to the lifeboat davits and

other handling equipment. The sleeping accommodations offer a greater variety of larger luxury cabins and suites, most of which are in the added midbody section and along the length of Deck 7, two levels below the main run of *topside* public facilities.

Below the waterline, the original *Vista* engine configuration with five diesel-alternators and an auxiliary gas turbine generator set was changed to an all-diesel-electric aggregate with the turbine's location in the forward engine room being taken up by the sixth diesel. The ship is propelled by two steerable engine pods suspended beneath the ship's stern. These do away with conventional long propeller shafts and the steel bossings that enclose them from where they protrude outside the hull to the propeller brackets beneath the stern. Without the need for these and the inherent inertia from them and power absorbed by their supporting thrust bearings and the watertight glands at their outer ends, a considerably smaller and more efficient modern electric motor can be housed directly inside the pod itself with a controllable-pitch propeller directly driven from its armature. As the pods are turnable, there is also no need for a heavy conventional rudder and its supporting stock.

Azipods, as these are called in an abbreviation of azimuthing pod, were first introduced aboard large passenger ships in 1998 with the *Carnival Elation*, second to last in their *Fantasy* series. These are now widely adopted throughout the cruise industry. The *Queen Mary 2* uses four of these, two azimuthing and two fixed to achieve her transatlantic service speed of 28.5 knots.

The *Queen Victoria*'s construction officially got underway with a keel laying ceremony held near Venice at the Marghera Yard of Italy's Fincantieri shipbuilders on 19th May 2006, when the first 325-ton section of the

*The **Queen Victoria**'s Grand Lobby is shown here from its forward stair landing between 2 and 3 Decks looking aft towards John McKenna's bronze bas relief of the ship. (Mike Louagie)*

ship's hull was lowered into position in the dry dock where she was to be assembled. The first steel had been cut and construction of the various blocks making up the hull and superstructure already started some months earlier. On 15th January 2007 the building dock was flooded and *Queen Victoria* floated free in her natural medium for the first time, being towed to the fitting-out dock for completion. During the final stages of her outfitting, sea trials were run in the Adriatic during August. The *Queen Victoria* was completed and handed over to Cunard on 24th November, in time to keep her appointment with the Duchess of Cornwall and Prince of Wales for her naming ceremony in Southampton on 10th December.[23]

Meanwhile the all-important task of designing the *Queen Victoria*'s numerous public spaces and individual accommodations was being co-ordinated and executed by the Genoese architect Giacomo Mortola and Teresa Anderson, architect and Vice President of Interior Design for Princess Cruises. With P&O Princess bringing another well-established and highly successful luxury cruise brand into the Carnival fold, care had to be taken to maintain the separate identities of both. Princess would continue to retain a more cosmopolitan international feel to its ships, while Cunard would develop the more traditional style of product to which it had long aspired.

With Princess having already built its *Sun* and *Grand* series in Italy, there was already continuity with Carnival's working relationship with Fincantieri and its design and technical departments. Anderson and Mortola had already designed the interiors for these and other Princess ships, and it was decided that the flexibility of their work was adaptable to also encompassing a suitable approach for the new Cunard

*The **Queen Victoria**, Grand Lobby's lighting scheme features a large art deco opal glass central ceiling lumiere surrounded by spotlights in an arrangement reflecting the curvilinear lines of the stairways and atrium space. (Mike Louagie)*

ship. At the same time, Anderson and Mortola were also to work with *QM2* architects SMC Design and Designteam on the interiors of the *Ventura* and *Azura*, as a modified version of the *Grand* series for the British-market P&O fleet.

Today's approach to designing interiors for the hospitality industry, including ships, is to create rather

43

FOR YOUR LEISURE & RELAXATION

1 Connexions™ Conference Centre (Deck 3)	11 Sea View Sauna - Cunard Royal Spa (Deck 9)
2 Cunard Royal Spa & Fitness Centre (Deck 9)	12 Sports Deck (Deck 11)
3 Cunardia Museum (Deck 2)	13 Royal Court Theatre (Decks 1, 2 & 3)
4 Empire Casino (Deck 2)	14 The Grand Lobby
5 Images (Deck 3)	15 The Royal Arcade - Shops (Deck 3)
6 Library (Decks 2 & 3)	16 The Terrace (Deck 11)
7 Hydropool - Cunard Royal Spa (Deck 9)	17 The Zone and Play Zone (Deck 10)
8 Lido Pool - Aft (Deck 9)	18 Whirlpools - Lido Pool - Aft (Deck 9)
9 Pavilion Pool (Deck 9)	19 Whirlpools - Pavilion Pool (Deck 9)
10 Queens Arcade (Deck 2)	20 The Grills Upper Terrace (Deck 12)

This plan of Queen Victoria reflects the traditional style used for Cunard Liners through the years

VICTORIA

DINING VENUES

| 21 | Britannia Restaurant (Decks 2 & 3) |

THE GRILLS

22	Princess Grill - Starboard Side (Deck 11)
23	Queens Grill - Port Side (Deck 11)
24	The Courtyard (Deck 11)
25	The Grills Lounge (Deck 11)

ALTERNATIVE DINING VENUES

26	Todd English Restaurant - Port Side (Deck 2)
27	Winter Garden - Retractable Roof (Deck 9)
28	Lido (Deck 9)

BARS & LOUNGES

29	Café Carinthia (Deck 2)
30	Chart Room (Deck 2)
31	Commodore Club (Deck 10)
32	Golden Lion (Deck 2)
33	Hemispheres (Deck 10)
34	Midships Bar and Lounge (Deck 3)
35	The Queens Room (Decks 2 & 3)
36	Churchill's Cigar Lounge (Deck 10)
37	Admiral's lounge (Deck 10)

Queen Victoria

CUNARD

*The **Queen Victoria**, a view into the Café Carinthia from the Royal Arcade alongside the Queen's Room mezzanine starboard on 3 Deck. (Mike Louagie)*

46

*The **Queen Victoria**, Cunard historical artefacts displayed in a vitrine on the Royal Arcade as part of the Cunard Heritage Trail. (Mike Louagie)*

than copy. Only an altogether new design scheme can make the best use of contemporary structures that enclose it, modern materials available to the designer and decorator, and above all the current living expectations of those who inhabit and use the spaces. A specific period style or other leitmotif can then be asserted within the scheme as a theatrical scenography to stimulate the desired atmosphere or ambience for the interior's use and enjoyment. The underlying *new scheme* takes into account the presence of the contemporary grid plan, technical facilities such as air-conditioning, wiring, plumbing, access for the handicapped,

emergency egress, and perhaps above all, modern architectural lighting.

The spaces themselves and their use are entirely different today – where the old *Queens* had a lounge, smoking room, library, card room and a small shop for each of their three passenger classes, today's passenger ships must provide elaborate theatres or cabaret lounges for staging full-production live entertainment, casinos and extensive shopping arcades, discotheques and alternative specialty restaurants, Internet cafés, as well as a vast array of sports and recreational facilities including elaborate spas, pools and lido decks never even

*The **Queen Victoria** underway at speed in the English Channel. (FotoFlite)*

*The **Queen Victoria**, looking into the signature Chart Room Bar from the Royal Arcade where it passes the Queen's Room mezzanine on 3 Deck. (Mike Louagie)*

*The **Queen Victoria**, another view of the Chart Room Bar which is arranged sidewalk-café style with only low balustrades separating it from the Royal Promenade and Queen's Room mezzanine, opposite. (Mike Louagie)*

*The **Queen Victoria** approaches her home berth in Southampton.*
(Andrew Cooke)

*The **Queen Victoria**'s Champagne Bar, now a Cunard signature feature first introduced aboard the **Queen Mary 2**, is adjacent to the Café Carinthia as seen in the background. (Mike Louagie)*

contemplated for liners built two or three generations ago. The decorative leitmotif added in ships built in our own times, even where these may reproduce items from, for instance the *Aquitania* or *Queen Mary*, is secondary to functionality and becomes largely a matter of detail.[24] In the end it is the detail, both in the architectural scheme itself and in added moveable and soft furnishings as well as the artwork that determines the ultimate quality of the finished scheme and perceived authenticity of its style.

While those of us old enough to recall details of the old Cunard *Queens* and other liners still in service during the 1960s, let alone the *Aquitania*, which was withdrawn from service in 1950, are a dwindling minority, these ships are nonetheless still well known to the general public. The great amount of publicity they attracted continues to flourish through countless books, films and other material about them, including the highly authentic reproduction of *Titanic* for Leonardo di Caprio's blockbuster 1997 motion picture of the same name. While a whimsical portrayal of these suffices on stage for a musical or theatrical production, or to some degree even in a mass-market hospitality or cruise ship setting, the sense of fidelity and authenticity demanded

*The **Queen Victoria** off the coast of Kent en route to Southampton. (FotoFlite)*

The **Queen Victoria**, *looking down the spiral staircase in the panelled warmth of the Library's lower level on Deck 2. (Mike Louagie)*

in the portrayal of these is highest in the premium upscale market that is served exclusively by Cunard and but a handful of others. The setting of a traditional theme in these circumstances must also go beyond mere architecture and design to also become part of the on-board experience with added touches of personal and individual service that are themselves appropriate to today's lifestyles and perceptions of exceptional service.

As part of the unique and memorable experience the *Queen Victoria* offers, passengers have the opportunity to learn the Olympic sport of foil fencing taught by qualified instructors from the British Fencing Association, with real swords and all the necessary safety and protective equipment provided for those wanting to participate. Most remarkably though, rather than being held in a gymnasium, fencing aboard the *Queen Victoria* is done in surroundings that more befit this elegant sport on the polished inlaid wood dance floor of the Queen's Room. Responding to the interest Cunard passengers have shown in learning and understanding through the Line's Connexions programme, operated in association with leading universities, theatrical performances and instructional workshops are given aboard the *Queen Victoria* by leading theatrical and professional groups.

The *Queen Victoria*'s designers made extensive studies of the old Cunard liners, the original *Queens*, *Aquitania* and *Mauretania* as well as other ships of relevant style such as the White Star Line's 1911 *Olympic*, a near contemporary of *Aquitania* and sister ship of *Titanic* and the lesser-known *Britannic* lost during World War I before she had any opportunity to go into commercial service. Steamship company brochures were used to get an idea also of how ships such as these were presented to the travelling public. Teresa Anderson also sought

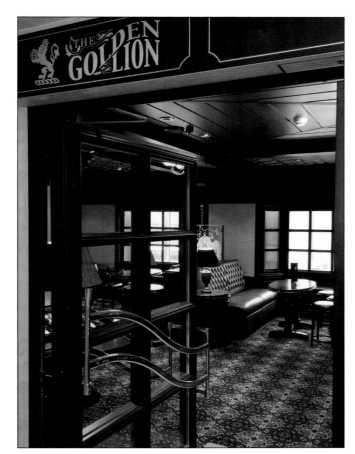

*The **Queen Victoria**, a glimpse from the Royal Arcade's lower court on 2 Deck into the Golden Lion Pub, a Cunard signature Public House feature first introduced in the mid 1990s aboard **QE2** and repeated aboard **QM2**. (Mike Louagie)*

references and inspiration from various hotels, private clubs and theatres in London, as well as country houses, National Trust and other heritage properties. Perhaps most significant among these was Queen Victoria and Albert's summer home, Osborne House, on the Isle of Wight.

57

*The **Queen Victoria**, the Queen's Room, decorated for the ship's inaugural Christmas season as seen from its rear entrance point off the Royal Arcade's lower gallery on 2 Deck. (Mike Louagie)*

*The **Queen Victoria**, the Queen's Room looking towards its starboard side with the galleries inspired by the Durbar Room in Osborne House. (Mike Louagie)*

While the *Queen Victoria* has a generous number of significant double and triple-height interiors, among them the library and shopping arcade, these needed to be given a unique treatment in the more traditional spirit of Cunard's background and the British establishments associated with it to differentiate these from the more contemporary feel of high-ceilinged spaces aboard other recently built upscale ships in the Holland America, Celebrity and P&O/Princess fleets. Here the designers have stressed art nouveau and deco references that can be rendered in the scale of these

spaces, along with the same genuine traditional materials and craftsmanship that graced Cunard interiors as much as a century ago, with wrought iron banister railings and a wide variety of *empire veneers* as these were called in the days of the old *Queens*, marble claddings and flooring. The fire-retardant veneers are especially made to meet today's stringent safety standards for shipboard use. The claddings are but a thin wafer of genuine Travertine marble bonded to a metal backing to reduce weight without compromising the stone's normal strength and rigidity.

59

The **Queen Victoria**'s alternative-dining Todd English restaurant, located port side of the Grand Lobby atrium on 2 Deck, follows the introduction of the Todd English experience aboard QM2. (Mike Louagie)

Among the *Queen Victoria*'s most notable interiors is the Grand Lobby that is the ship's main entrance and principal atrium, extending up from Deck 1 through the two levels of main public rooms above. It is here that embarking passengers get their all-important first impression of the ship and the voyage they are about to enjoy aboard her. The grand staircase leading to the deck above is inspired by the *Olympic*'s oak and wrought iron staircase where it's uppermost flights ascended from a glass-domed mezzanine-plan hall forward of the first class public rooms to the boat deck above. The *Olympic* stairway's already dramatic effect is enhanced and brought up to the *Queen Victoria*'s larger scale, with the place of a grotto and clock on the wall above its landing taken in the new ship by a large Roman arch extending two-and-a-half decks up from the stair landing to the atrium's ceiling surrounding a deco-style bronze bas-relief of the ship on a globe with a compass rose at its base and radiant sunburst above.

Created by artist John McKenna, this and a similar work in the atrium aboard the *Queen Mary 2* are inspired by MacDonald Gill's famous map mural with its clock, sunburst and tiny animated models of the *Queens* showing their positions on the North Atlantic that adorns the old *Queen Mary*'s main dining room to this day in her now static role in Long Beach, California. To achieve the effect of this, the stairway connecting the atrium's two upper levels is cantilevered above the forward end of the atrium opening from where the scene can be enjoyed from various heights. Above, the atrium is crowned by a shallow dome with a large central deco-style glass light fixture.

On boarding the *Queen Victoria* one becomes immediately immersed into warm hues of the Grand Lobby's rich mahogany panelling, the earth tones of its carpeting and upholstered furnishings in the glow of electric light filtered through the dome's opal glass fixtures and from accenting spotlights. It is a sensation that evokes first impressions of the old Cunard *Queens*, and for the vast majority of passengers today who have never experienced this first hand, at least the same feeling is conveyed by all those remarkable sepia-tone photographs of these ships that have stirred their imaginations through the last three generations.

Forward of the Grand Lobby's upper two levels and beyond the Queen's Room, the Royal Arcade, also panelled in rich veneers and with wrought-iron balustrades is inspired by London's classically chic Burlington and Queen's Opera Arcades, with the bay-windowed design of its shop fronts reflecting the classic style of these elegant London passages. The central open atrium area and processional staircase, however, also show the influence of the 1920s and 1930s mezzanine-

*The **Queen Victoria**, diaphanous curtain swags lend an added sense of intimacy to the tables along the Todd English restaurant's port side outer wall. (Mike Louagie)*

*The **Queen Victoria**, a partial view of the Britannia Restaurant, looking along the room's starboard side. (Mike Louagie)*

plan ocean liner ballrooms and lounges. The majority of shops are arranged around the mezzanine, following a similar plan from the *QE2*'s Double Room upper level so rearranged as part of her first major refit in 1972. The Royal Arcade's lower level encompasses the Empire Casino, with the Golden Lion Pub enclosed under the starboard mezzanine. Here, at the centre of the stairway, is a standard clock with Westminster Chimes from Dent & Company who made the great four-faced tower clock of the Houses of Parliament in Westminster whose famed Big Ben bell has chimed the hours in London for more than 130 years, and is internationally known to

radio listeners of BBC World Service.

The Queen's Room has now become an institution aboard Cunard's ships, following its appearance first aboard the *QE2* as her first-class main lounge. Brought forward both to the *QM2* and now to the *Queen Victoria*, this serves mainly as a hotel-style ballroom for the "black and white" balls with gentlemen attired in tuxedos or dinner jackets and ladies in formal long gowns that reflect the British love of ballroom dancing and have also become a prominent feature of the social life aboard Cunard's ships. With the flat surface of a large dance floor, a stage and ample seating, the Queen's Room

*The **Queen Victoria** looking into the Britannia Restaurant from its entrances on 2 and 3 Deck, one has a vista of the room's double-height central nave and the art déco sculptured centrepiece behind the Captain's table. (Mike Louagie)*

63

The **Queen Victoria**'s double-height Royal Arcade court looking forward from in front of the casino (to the left out of view) towards its processional staircase and Big Ben standard clock. (Mike Louagie)

serves a variety of other functions for everything from receptions, daytime entertainment, afternoon tea, fashion shows and parties, to passport inspection, immigration formalities and other such processing of passengers where these are carried out aboard ship prior to disembarkation. On other ships these procedures all too often have to be handled in cabaret lounges where passengers must queue on sloped or terraced floors and then ascend stairs to the stage proscenium for processing.

The *Queen Victoria*'s Queen's Room draws inspiration from Osborne House, where the colonnaded loggia and upper gallery along the room's starboard and aft sides is inspired by similar features forming a loggia and musicians' gallery along one side of the palace's ornate Durbar Room, its name derived from the Hindi word *darbar*, meaning court. Designed as a state banquet hall and ballroom, the Indian themed Durbar Room is part of the new *Main Wing*, housing accommodations for the

*The **Queen Victoria**, a close-up view of the Royal Arcade's clock inspired by the timepiece in the Houses of Parliament tower at Westminster, and made by London clockmakers Dent & Company especially for the ship. (Mike Louagie)*

Royal household, council and audience added to the house in 1890-91. The reference to Osborne House is very appropriate for the new Cunard ship, as it was Queen Victoria's favourite residence from the time of its acquisition early in her reign until she returned to the Isle of Wight to live out the last days of her long and illustrious life.

The Queen's Room is adorned with a portrait of Victoria as the young Queen-Empress painted by Italian-born New York artist Giancarlo Impiglia, already familiar for his works aboard Cunard's other *Queens*. Most notable among these are his more abstract contemporary brightly colourful depictions of life aboard imaginary cruise ships in murals aboard the *QE2* and *QM2*. His latest work aboard the *Queen Victoria* is quite different from these in that it is a more scholarly

*The **Queen Victoria**, another view of the Royal Arcade Court, seen here from the 3 Deck gallery. (Mike Louagie)*

*The **Queen Victoria**, performers and stage crew prepare for an evening show in the ship's Royal Court Theatre, itself a virtually full-scale London theatre extending up through the height of 1, 2 and 3 Decks. (Mike Louagie)*

The **Queen Victoria**, inside the glass-roofed Winter Garden looking towards the ship's starboard side, with part of the open-air Pavilion Pool lido visible through the sliding doors to the left. (Mike Louagie)

67

*The **Queen Victoria**, appearing as though ready for the start of a race, exercise cycles are lined up in the Cunard Health Club and Spa on 9 Deck ready to be used by fitness-conscious passengers. (Mike Louagie)*

nineteenth-century-style portrait from an age before photography rather than the situation depictions where the characters are virtually featureless. Impiglia made a thorough study of nineteenth-century portraits of the young Victoria enabling him to develop an entirely new image of her for his work, which is itself a return to the time of his own art studies in Rome.[25]

Apart from its architectural references to the Durbar Room's loggia and gallery, decoration of the *Queen Victoria*'s Queen's Room is generally of a light and elegant liner style, perhaps recalling ocean-going styles of the 1930s, with its use of light maple veneers, gold-leaf ornamentation and back-lit stained-glass murals. Designed as a primarily inside space, flanked by the Royal Gallery's extension on one side and with windows in the opposite ship's side only on its main level, the two large crystal chandeliers above the dance floor are the main light source, along with the indirect lighting of the

*The **Queen Victoria**'s aft swimming pool on 9 Deck seen against the Rotterdam cityscape. (Mike Louagie)*

*The **Queen Victoria**'s Pavilion Pool and lido amidships on 9 Deck, showing its adjacency to the Winter Garden, left in the photo. (Mike Louagie)*

*The **Queen Victoria**, a soup servery in the Lido Restaurant on 9 Deck, showing the room's decorative tiled wall paintings. (Mike Louagie)*

69

*The **Queen Victoria**, a vintage painting of Cunard's first **Mauretania** (1907-35) with her hull in "cruising white" of her latter years in service adorned a wall in the Churchill's Admiral's Lounge on 10 Deck. (Mike Louagie)*

coffered ceiling surrounding them. The raised seating areas in the loggias to either side of the dance floor and the starboard side gallery above are arranged for optimum viewing of the large dance floor in a style, recalling the Grand Hotel experience of a century ago as it would have been in the Dorchester or London Ritz Carlton.

Across the forward end of Decks 1, 2 and 3 is the Royal Court Theatre, serving as the *Queen Victoria*'s main entertainment venue. Unlike many American-based cruise ships where the main show place is in fact a Las Vegas-style cabaret lounge, designed for revue-style variety shows, with cocktail tables and bar service provided for the audience, the 830-seat Royal Court Theatre is styled after the London West End and Broadway commercial theatres of the early twentieth century, geared to a lighter genre of dramatic, comedic and music-hall shows aimed at the broader spectrum of the population in large cities such as London and New York.[26]

A key feature of the Royal Court Theatre's ornately decorated auditorium is the inclusion of 16 private boxes at its two upper levels. Apart from the novelty of offering a feature such as this at sea, is the way in which those booking the boxes are given a special experience when attending the performance. The idea is for them to be personally escorted by the ship's liveried bellboys from the restaurant after dinner to special reception lounges behind the boxes at either side of the theatre for dessert and pre-show champagne before being ushered to their private boxes. It is touches such as these that, as much as anything else, contribute to the passenger's real sense of an exclusive luxury cruise experience.[27] Unreserved boxes are made available to others on a first-come-first-served basis immediately before the show.

The **Queen Victoria**, *a corner of the Churchill's Cigar Lounge, showing the room's individual pedestal tables and traditional leather-upholstered smoking-room chairs. (Mike Louagie)*

71

*The **Queen Victoria**'s Commodore Club offers panoramic views forward and to either side of the ship from the forward end of 10 Deck, a full two decks above the navigating bridge. (Mike Louagie)*

*The **Queen Victoria**, the domed circular Hemispheres lounge on 10 Deck is one of the ship's more modern and high tech spaces. (Mike Louagi*

The **Queen Victoria**, *seen here is the Princess Grill restaurant, located highest in the ship at the funnel's base on 11 Deck, looking aft inside the room.* (Mike Louagie)

*The **Queen Victoria**, another view of the Princess Grill interior at the room's forward end. (Mike Louagie)*

The Library, tucked in behind the port-side lifts amidships, is one of the ship's smaller double-decker spaces, with its mezzanine plan, open spiral staircase and backlit stained-glass dome at its centre. It bears the design influence of London's many exclusive private clubs, or perhaps even the academic surroundings of a college at Oxford or Cambridge Universities. Apart from the split-level arrangement of the old *Queen Elizabeth*'s library, this is the only Cunard ship to have a multi-level library, and is rivalled in today's cruise fleets only by Celebrity's *Millennium* series ships. The *Queen Victoria*'s Library's collection of 6,000 volumes is supplemented with audio books and other modern electronic media.

The main Britannia Restaurant at the aft end of Decks 2 and 3 follows the overall *Vista* layout, with panoramic windows on three sides, though with a

*The **Queen Victoria**, a standard-grade Britannia veranda stateroom. (Cunard)*

*The **Queen Victoria**, a Princess-grade Grills veranda suite. (Cunard)*

smaller opening between its upper and lower levels so as to increase the dining area itself. Upon entering the room one has an axial vista along its double-height nave towards a large deco sculpture in bronze and glass of Cunard's rampant lion and the globe from the Line's house flag, set into a freestanding panel as a backdrop to the Captain's table. The style of this too is reminiscent of MacDonald Gill's mural in the old *Queen Mary*'s first-class dining room. Without being exclusively of any particular style, the room is otherwise representative of various influences evoking the liner era and age of grand luxe travel as a background setting for enjoyment of the *Queen Victoria*'s gastronomy. While many cruise lines in the standard market are moving away from formal dining with fixed table assignments and meal times, Cunard continues to stress a single sitting for lunch and dinner times, and assigned table seating fostering a more personal relationship between passengers and the

restaurant staff who thus look after them throughout the voyage.

As aboard the *QM2* those occupying premium-grade cabins and suites are served in the exclusive Princess and Queen's Grill restaurants located on their own deck high above the ship, along with the private Grill Lounge. These rooms all offer a panoramic outlook from full-height widows looking out to the horizon at either side, and forward over the ship's open decks below. They are grouped around a small central enclosed court, open to the sky above where outdoor alfresco service is available in warm weather.

The *Queen Victoria* reflects Cunard's strong emphasis on food and beverage services, firmly rooted in Cunard's traditional liner services. During the earlier liner era when, apart from ballroom dancing to music played by the ship's orchestra and improvised film shows in the lounge, passengers otherwise were left to their own

The **Queen Victoria**, a view into the Grill Terrace court located between the Princess and Queen's Grill restaurants looking towards the Princess Grill to starboard. (Mike Louagie)

devices to pass the long days at sea. Meal times were thus events of the day to be looked forward to as much as for being significant social occasions as for enjoyment of the gastronomy itself. Cunard has long prided itself on the quality and variety its cuisine – a passenger's request for bacon at breakfast on the old *Queens*, for instance, would bring the inevitable steward's response, "What kind Sir / Madam" – there were three to choose from. Dining aboard the *Queen Mary 2* and *Queen Victoria* is still special among the broader range of activities and diversions these ships offer, reflecting the current trends of five-star hotelier haut cuisine, featuring both British and international specialties.

The emphasis is as much on diversity as it is on the quality of food and service. The Britannia Restaurant retains the traditional liner era institution of a formal à-la-carte dinner service each evening with two fixed sittings, though with breakfast and lunch offered on a more informal open seating basis. Alternatively, passengers can dine al fresco in the Lido Café at breakfast and lunch times and choose a reserved-seating bistro-style evening dining experience featuring cuisine from different parts of the world each evening. Traditional British *pub grub* such as fish and chips, toad in the hole and bangers and mash, never offered aboard the old *Queens*, is featured in the Golden Lion Pub, from its own kitchen with the necessary deep fryers and other equipment for this culinary genre. At the higher end of the scale is the exclusive cover-charge Todd English Restaurant serving the renowned American celebrity chef's nouveau and Mediterranean cuisine in the characteristic opulence of his establishments ashore.

Dining aboard the *Queen Victoria* also retains a vestigial legacy of the three-class service aboard the old Cunard *Queens*, though here it is in effect first class, first plus and first plus plus, based on the wide range of cabin and suite grades. The Queen's and Princess's Grill Restaurants cater exclusively at two levels to those occupying the ship's premium-grade cabins and suites. In addition to the impeccable à la carte service and individual cuisine of these restaurants, passengers in the "Grill" classes can dine al fresco in the sheltered open-air courtyard between the two Grill restaurants.

Also among the *Queen Victoria*'s upper decks public rooms is the Commodore Club overlooking the ship's bow from a vantage point high above the navigating bridge, offering the same compelling vistas over the ship's bow as did the forward-facing cocktail bars aboard Cunard's old *Queens* three-quarters of a century ago. The *Queen Mary 2* introduced the Commodore Club as a more contemporary take on this, reflecting the *QE2*'s original Look Out Lounge before it disappeared as a victim of her 1972 refit. Despite its modern features of wraparound panoramic windows on three sides and raised central bar area for optimum advantage of the outlook, this newest interpretation goes back to even earlier traditions in its decoration and furnishings, with high-back winged club chairs leather upholstery, brass fittings and rich dark veneers. It is adjoined by the similarly styled Admiral's Club and Churchill's Cigar Lounge. Aft of these and the forward main stair-tower is the circular-plan Hemispheres, serving as both a flexible venue for various daytime activities, before becoming an elegant nightclub after dark. With its perforated bright metal sphere set into a sectioned glazed screen at the room's entrance, providing both privacy and a central focal point to the interior, this is probably the most contemporary public space aboard the *Queen Victoria*.

*The **Queen Victoria** emerges through early-morning fog, brand new on her first in-service port of call at Rotterdam Europoort on 12th December 2007. (Mike Louagie)*

79

CHAPTER 3

THE QUEEN VICTORIA MAKES HER DEBUT

CUNARD

QUEEN VICTORIA

At 11:00 am on 24th November 2007, the Italian flag was lowered from the *Queen Victoria*'s mast and the Red Ensign run up in its place while the ship changed nationality and ownership as she was officially handed over from her builders to her owners at Fincantieri's Marghera yard. Later that day, after the dignitaries and guests invited for the handover had left and final preparations for sea were completed, the second largest ship ever built for Cunard after the *Queen Mary 2* sailed for her new home and port of registry at Southampton, arriving there a week later to be prepared for her official naming ceremony and service debut.

Naming ceremonies have now taken the place of traditional launchings, when she would be named by some prominent person, usually a lady, chosen to do the honours. A bottle of champagne would be swung by hand against the bow, and as it shattered, a lever pulled to, symbolically at least, release the launch mechanism setting hull in motion, sliding down from its inclined building ways into the water as thousands of shipyard workers cheered and tossed their caps into the air. These events were always a dramatic celebration of human industrial endeavour that, alas, has since given way to the rationale of more modern ways.

Today's ships are block-built from already-assembled sections of the hull and superstructure weighing several

*The **Queen Victoria** is given a traditional fireboat welcome on her maiden approach to Southampton Docks as she arrives in England from Fincantieri. (Andrew Cooke)*

*The **Queen Victoria** lies alongside the City Cruise Terminal in the Port of Southampton's Western Docks in readiness for her naming ceremony. (Andrew Cooke)*

hundred tons apiece that are precisely aligned along the bottom of a dry dock and attached to one another by automated electric-arc-welding equipment. The *baptism* comes when the ship is floated free as the dock is flooded and she is manoeuvred by tugs to a fitting-out quay for the completion of her upper decks and funnel and other outer structures, the *stepping* of her main mast and outfitting of her interiors. The floating out is usually marked by a small shipyard ceremony, with the traditional launch celebration in effect replaced by a

naming ceremony performed at the new ship's home port after she is completed and handed over to her owners. The already-known name is unveiled by the ship's *Godmother*, as the officiating lady is now known, and a jeroboam of champagne shattered against the hull plating. The poignancy of such celebrations today is heightened by a sense of the ship's *belonging* to the home port, from where she will sail, and where there is a sense of her belonging to the town or city and its populace, some of whom probably at least will sail with her as

*The **Queen Victoria** is swung by the tug **Svitzer Sarah** in readiness to go alongside Pier 101 at the City Cruise Terminal. (Andrew Cooke)*

officers and crew.

The *Queen Victoria*'s naming ceremony in Southampton occurred almost four years after the same honours were performed there for her French-built older sister the *Queen Mary 2*. The venue was, however, changed from the Ocean Dock to the City Cruise Terminal, where spectators would have a better view of the ship and the outdoor festivities from nearby Mayflower Park, where they would be unencumbered by security restrictions on access to the port itself.

A full day of festivities both ashore and on board was highlighted by the 3:30 pm naming ceremony itself. This was held in a large temporary auditorium erected on the quayside with terraced seating to optimise viewing for 2,000 invited guests and the stage backdrop being a glass wall through which the ship's bow could be seen. The ship was first blessed by the Bishop of Winchester with the words:

"They that go down to the sea in ships;
That do business in great waters;
These see the works of the Lord, and His wonders in
the deep."

The naming itself was performed by HRH Duchess of Cornwall, accompanied by her husband HRH The Prince of Wales, with the traditional phrases:

"I name this ship Queen Victoria; May God bless all who
sail upon her".

The Duchess then pressed a button to release a magnum of Veuve Clicquot that hit the *Queen Victoria*'s port side shell plating on target but remained intact. As things such as this do happen at namings, someone was standing by with a reserve bottle that was quickly thrust down from the bow deck and did shatter with the desired effect as the *Queen Victoria*'s whistle bellowed overhead and helium-filled balloons were released into

Cunard CEO, Carol Marlow, HRH The Prince of Wales and his wife the HRH Duchess of Cornwall at the naming ceremony. (Cunard)

*The **Queen Victoria** is honoured with a spectacular firework display as she leaves Southampton on her maiden voyage. (Cunard)*

the air, also to the tumultuous applause and cheers of the official quayside party and the additional thousands who had thronged into Mayflower Park.

The ceremony also included the London Philharmonic Orchestra accompanying singer Katherine Jenkins in selections from Bizet's Carmen, and the three tenors, Alfie Boe, Jon Christos and Gardar Thor Cortes finishing up with a patriotic rendition of Rule Britannia.

Cunard has retained a long-standing relationship with the Royal Family. The *Queen Mary* was launched on 26th September 1934 by her Royal namesake (1867-1953) and the *Queen Elizabeth* on 27th September 1938 by hers, Elizabeth the late Queen Mother (1900-2002). Both ships were visited on various occasions during their long careers by the Queens who had launched them, though. HM Queen Elizabeth II launched the *Queen Elizabeth 2*

85

*The **Queen Victoria**, opera singer Katherine Jenkins in performance at the concert that followed the ship's naming ceremony. (Cunard)*

on 20th September 1967 and named the *Queen Mary 2* on 8th January 2004. She and the Duke of Edinburgh have visited the *QE2* at various times during her career with a final tour of the ship being made by Prince Philip on the day of her departure from Southampton to her new owners in Dubai.

Prince Charles was on the bridge of the *QE2* with Cunard chairman, Sir Basil Smallpiece and Captain William Warwick 19th November 1968 when the ship departed from her Clydeside fitting-out berth under her own steam for drydocking at Greenock. His first wife HRH Princess Diana named the Finnish-built cruise ship *Royal Princess* for P&O Princess Cruises at Southampton in 1984, and in 1987 toured the *QE2*, hosted a children's event on board and met with crew members from all departments following the ship's re-engining refit in Germany.

As the last guests of the naming ceremonies

*The **Queen Victoria** is illuminated by a glint of sunlight across her side from between Manhattan's skyscrapers as she makes an early morning arrival in New York City. (Cunard)*

*The **Queen Victoria** alongside in Southampton's Western Docks as the **Queen Mary 2** makes her departure in the foreground. (Cunard)*

disembarked from the *Queen Victoria* the following morning, the final consignments of stores were already going aboard as the ship was made ready for work. Paying passengers embarked later that day for her first voyage, a ten-day Christmas Markets cruise to Rotterdam, Copenhagen, Oslo, Hamburg and Zeebrugge. The opportunity was taken to also showcase the *Queen Victoria* to the European media and travel industry with tours of the ship, briefings, luncheons and other events arranged at each port of call. This was followed by a Christmas cruise to Madeira and the

Canary Islands. Coincidentally when, after 27 years on the North Atlantic and in wartime service, the old *Queen Mary* made her first cruise on 23rd December 1963, this too was a round-trip Christmas excursion to the Atlantic Islands from Southampton.

On 6th January 2008 the *Queen Victoria* began her first around-the-world cruise, a 106-day westwards-about circumnavigation of the globe, first to New York, through the Panama Canal to Los Angeles, onwards to Hawaii, the South Pacific, South East Asia, India, Dubai, Egypt and through Suez to the Mediterranean and back

Left: The **Queen Victoria**, *seen here underway at speed shortly after her completion. (Cunard)*

Above: The **Queen Victoria**, *in the background departs from Sydney Harbour as the* **Queen Elizabeth 2** *arrives on one of her last visits to Australia. (Cunard)*

home to Southampton. The first leg of the voyage, a direct winter North Atlantic crossing to New York was made in tandem with, and also under the perhaps motherly watch of, the veteran *QE2*. Both *Queens* arrived in New York on 13th January, where they were joined by the *Queen Mary 2* for the first-ever rendezvous of three Cunard *Queens*. The event was feted with a spectacular fireworks display against a backdrop of the Manhattan skyline and the Statue of Liberty.

The *Queen Victoria* and *QE2* were to meet again for the last time on 19th July 2008, when the two ships tied up bow to bow at Zeebrugge. The *QE2*'s sale to Istithmar investment group for redevelopment as a hotel and tourist attraction in the Palm Jumeirah beach complex in Dubai had already been announced on 18th June 2007, and the ship was halfway through her last season with Cunard. As passengers gazed up at both ships from the pier, groups of crew members from each visited those aboard the other.

At the time of writing these closing paragraphs of this book, the *Queen Victoria* has been service almost five years to the day. In Cunard's tradition of swift, regular and safe passage, she has performed without incident or mishap and has already become a successful and popular ship. She is a modern ship functionally and operationally, and is endowed with a strong sense of tradition in the style with which Cunard identifies itself.

As Christopher Rynd, who has commanded the *Queen Elizabeth 2*, *Queen Mary 2* and *Queen Victoria* explains, those of Cunard's loyal following who came to the *Queen Victoria* with the feeling that nothing could ever compare with their beloved *QE2* are pleased and well satisfied with the experience the new ship offers.[28]

*The **Queen Elizabeth** joined the **Queen Victoria** in October 2010. (Brian Smith)*

*The **Queen Victoria** departing from Venice in a painting by Robert Lloyd.*

*The **Queen Victoria** approaching the Wilhelminapier dock on Rotterdam's revitalised Suidkade. (Mike Louagie)*

REFERENCES

1   Author interview with Andy Collier, SMC Design, London, 11th May 2001

2   At about this time Cunard had adopted a fairly aggressive strategy of promoting their ships as being *iconic*, trading on the unique status of the Line's flagship *Queen Elizabeth 2*

3   Palmer & Colton, *A History of the Modern World*, p. 426

4   Cunard had already started using screw-propelled ships in their Mediterranean trades from the early 1850s

5   Bonsor, *North Atlantic Seaway*, p. 17

6   "The UK population, past, present and future," http://statistics.gov.uk

7   Hughes, *The Blue Riband of the Atlantic*, p. 49

8   Rowland, *Steam at Sea*, p. 172

9   Holland, *Travellers' Architecture*, p. 44, 46
The Paddington Hotel, now the Paddington Hilton, continues to flourish, and the St. Pancras Hotel, later known as the Midland Grand, and then closed for many years, is being restored as a luxury residence and Marriott Hotel as part of the St. Pancras Station redevelopment scheme.

10 Hughes, *The Blue Riband of the Atlantic*, p. 73

11 Hughes, *The Blue Riband of the Atlantic*, p. 84

12 Benstead, *Atlantic Ferry*, p. 27

13 Wealeans, *Designing Liners*, p. 53

14 Wealeans, *Designing Liners*, p. 46

15 Benstead, *Atlantic Ferry*, p. 27

16 The Deutsche Werkbund (German Work Federation) was an organization of designers, artists, engineers and industrialists whose aim was to establish working relationships between art and industry.

17 Heskett, *Industrial Design*, p. 92

18 *The Architects' Journal*, 25th January 1934

19 BBC Scotland television documentary *QE2: The last great liner*, 2007

20 Agnew, *The Architectural Review*, June 1969, p. 412

21 Casson, *The Times*, Special QE2 Supplement, Tuesday 29th April, 1969

22 *Cruise & Ferry Info*, January 2006, p. 24

23 Schwerdtner, *Die Neuen Queens der Cunard Line*, p. 161-4

24 Dawson, *ShipPax Guide 99*, p. 76

25 Wagner, *The Porthole*, p. 7

26 Sharp, *The Architectural Review*, London, June 1989, p. 24

27 Wagner, *The Log*, Navy League of the United States, New York Council, July 2007

28 Wagner, Beyondships.com, September 2008

*The **Queen Victoria**, looking up to the Grand Lobby ceiling with its great domed art deco light fixture and the surrounding array of other spotlights that bring this virtually inner entire space to life. (Mike Louagie)*

The **Queen Victoria**, *a painting by Robert Lloyd showing the ship against a background of the Venice waterfront.*

94

QUEEN VICTORIA - CUNARD LINE, SOUTHAMPTON

FotoFlite

Builders:	Fincantieri, Marghera Yard, Italy
Keel laid:	16th May 2006
Floated out:	15th January 2007
Delivered:	24th November 2007
Fincantieri Yard number:	6127
IMO number:	9320556
Flag:	United Kingdom
Port of registry:	Southampton
Classification:	Lloyd's Register +100A1

Overall dimensions

Length overall:	294.0 m
Waterline length:	265.36 m
Beam:	32.36 m
Draft:	7.9 m
Air draft (Height above waterline):	55.07 m
Depth to bulkhead deck (A Deck):	10.80 m
Depth to Promenade Deck (3 Deck):	19.81 m

Measure and capacities

Gross tonnage (GT):	90,049
Net tonnage (NT):	50,125
Deadweight tonnage (tDW):	7,700
Passengers, lower berths:	2,014
Passengers, maximum:	2,144 including fold-away upper berths and settee beds
Passenger accommodations:	1,007 cabins and suites, 86% with outside exposure, 71% with private verandas

Officers and crew:	818 in 528 cabins
Fuel capacity:	3,456 m²
Fresh water capacity:	3,150 m²

Machinery and performance

Power:	6 diesel generator sets in total generating 63,380 kW of electrical power.
Propulsion:	2 azimuthing propeller pods yielding a total motive power of 35,200 kW
Trial speed:	24.3 knots
Service speed:	21.7 knots
Fuel consumption:	240 tones heavy fuel oil per 24 hours
Manoeuvering:	2 transverse bow thrusters used in conjunction with the pods for docking
Stabilization:	2 retractable anti-rolling fins

ACKNOWLEDGEMENTS

Mike Louagie

The author and publishers wish to extend their sincere thanks to all those who have helped with the preparation of this book and with bringing it into reality. A work such as this is only possible with the whole-hearted support and collaboration of the owners and the builders, with our special thanks to Peter Shanks and Michael Gallagher of Cunard and Fincantieri's Marghera Yard. We are especially grateful to the photographers whose outstanding work gives this book its remarkable graphic impact. Thanks to Mike Louagie for his ever-outstanding interior photography of the *Queen Victoria* herself and the views of her from Rotterdam, as well as to Andrew Cooke for his coverage from Southampton, and to John Hendy for historical and other images, as well as to FotoFlite and Brian Smith. There are also those who contribute by way of enthusiastically sharing their background and historical knowledge, technical and industry expertise, with our special thanks going to Klas Brogren of ShipPax Information, Stephen Payne of Carnival Corporate Shipbuilding, John and Diana Lang of The Cruise People Limited, Toronto, and to my fellow author, ship and design expert Bruce Peter of the Glasgow School of Art.

On a personal note the author especially wishes to thank Miles and Linda Cowsill of Ferry Publications for all of their kindness and cooperation in putting this delightful book together.

We trust that our readers will enjoy this work as much as it is our pleasure to put it together for them.